Vocabulary, Corpus and Language Teaching

Muthyala Udaya • Chada Ramamuni Reddy
Editors

Vocabulary, Corpus and Language Teaching

A Machine-Generated Literature Overview

Springer

Editors
Muthyala Udaya
Armsburg Alluri Apartments, Flat 403
Hyderabad, Telangana, India

Chada Ramamuni Reddy
Department of ESL Studies
English and Foreign Languages University
Hyderabad, Telangana, India

ISBN 978-3-031-45985-6 ISBN 978-3-031-45986-3 (eBook)
https://doi.org/10.1007/978-3-031-45986-3

The translation was done with the help of an artificial intelligence machine translation tool. A subsequent human revision was done primarily in terms of content.

This Springer imprint is published by the registered company Springer Nature Switzerland AG
The registered company address is: Gewerbestrasse 11, 6330 Cham, Switzerland

Paper in this product is recyclable.

Introduction

Auto-summaries can be generated by either an abstractive or extractive auto-summarization:

- *An extraction-based summarizer identifies the most important sentences of a text and uses the original sentences to create the summary.*
- *An abstraction-based summarizer creates new text based on deep learning. New phrases are created to summarize the content.*

The auto-summaries you will find in this book have been generated via an extractive summarization approach.

Each chapter was carefully edited by Udaya M and Ramamuni Reddy C. The editors selected the papers which were then auto-summarized. The editors have not edited the auto-summaries due to the extraction-based approach and have not changed the original sentences. You will find the editors' reviews and guidance on the auto-summaries in their chapter introductions.

In machine-generated books, editors are defined as those who curate the content for the book by selecting the papers to be auto-summarized and by organizing the output into a meaningful order. Next to the thoughtful curation of the papers, editors should guide the readers through the auto-summaries and make transparent why they selected the papers.

The ultimate goal is to provide a current literature review of Springer Nature publications on a given topic in order to support readers in overcoming information overload and to help them dive into a topic faster, to identify interdisciplinary overlaps, and to present papers which might not have been on the readers' radar.

Please note that the selected papers are not used to train an Large Language Models (LLM) while the auto-summaries are created.

Contents

Chapter 1
Introduction

In the modern world, innovation is one of the main driving forces of economic and social development. AI research and development technologies have a special place in the science world since they help solve many problems. In particular, AI & Ml resolve one of the most critical issues for researchers: data analysis. As huge amounts of data make it difficult to find relevant information necessary for researchers, AI quickly solves such issues with a single search and extracts patterns. It helps researchers discover data similarities; it helps make decisions by revealing insights that scientists have missed. Artificial intelligence and machine learning appeared in the middle of the last century. In recent years, thanks to the emergence of new fundamental techniques, the availability of huge amounts of accumulated data, and the development of hardware capacities, interest in this technology has reached its peak. Machine-generated literature overviews are automatically generated summaries of already published SN research publications. The algorithm identifies relations between articles and chapters and clusters the summaries into a table of contents. The summaries in orient themselves on the original structure of the chapters and articles, which means you can also have small summaries of each subsection.

This book attempts to help ESL/EFL researchers and teachers understand the domain of vocabulary instruction in the field of language education and learning. Vocabulary is the core of language, and words are important to a typical language learner. Nonetheless, researchers and teachers in the field of language acquisition undervalued the role of vocabulary by prioritising syntax or phonology, which are central to linguistic theory and more critical to language pedagogy. Therefore, in recent years, ESL/EFL vocabulary acquisition has become an increasingly interesting topic for researchers, teachers, curriculum designers, theorists, and others involved in language teaching and learning.

The chapters in this book are grouped together to provide balanced research coverage and help young researchers activate their knowledge in less time. The preface provides a framework for the rest of the book by introducing the main aspects: Vocabulary and acquisition; vocabulary teaching and learning strategies;

M. Udaya, C. R. Reddy (eds.), *Vocabulary, Corpus and Language Teaching*,
https://doi.org/10.1007/978-3-031-45986-3_1

vocabulary information technology for vocabulary learning; corpus-based vocabulary research; and current practises are some of the topics covered in this book. In doing so, it emphasises the sub-topics that have received the most attention in the literature: (1) Discussions of various vocabulary acquisition teaching methods; (2) Different types of vocabulary enhancement teaching and learning strategies; (3) Integrating ICT in vocabulary teaching to promote better learning; and (4) Corpus studies with functional references.

Second or Foreign Language Vocabulary Acquisition will be of great interest to those interested in current views on the nature of L1-L2 vocabulary acquisition and approaches to vocabulary instruction. Based on these criteria, the summaries presented in part I focus on various aspects such as self-efficacy beliefs and academic achievement, with instructional interventions demonstrating that learning strategies enhance task-related cognitive sets. Another study focused on English morphological awareness plays an important role in French vocabulary acquisition because L1 plays an important role in L2 acquisition. According to Wysocki and Jenkins' (1987) research on morphological generality, increasing vocabulary size leads to a higher level of abstract morphological perception than base and suffix recognition, especially for sixth and eighth graders. Additionally few studies found that writing morphology aids in recognising meaning cues in complex words and enriches the vocabulary of fourth and fifth graders. Krashens' monitor model also helps in understanding incomprehensible inputs and the ability to successfully translate foreign words and generate situational models for understanding. Future research may aim to determine the optimal number of spell exposures required to ensure adequate knowledge of words in memory.

In Part II the contrast to "GroupLens" collaborative filtering algorithm, Estrand et al.'s (2010) collaborative filtering theory focuses on making and testing vocabulary learning tools, which are a powerful way for users to sort through large amounts of information and goods. The teaching and learning of languages in a setting that makes use of technology is a useful alternative to conventional education. Depending on the way they are taught, when students read new texts, books, poems, articles, or other materials, they use different strategies to learn new words. These strategies assist in teacher and peer-scaffolding from a sociocultural perspective, resulting in the application of collaborative techniques (scaffolding). To add, one important strategy is metacognition, which has two aspects: knowledge of cognition (i.e., to know what, how, when, and why to use strategies); and regulation of cognition: metacognitive control strategies, such as goal-setting, self-monitoring, and self-evaluation [1]. Few studies discussed how learners' needs are involved in cognitive VLS and how to enhance their awareness of and mastery of metacognition. All the teaching techniques are covered here, along with some intriguing ideas on self-regulation. The focus is on students' self-initiation, or their own deliberate efforts to control their learning process [2]. Instead of just teaching cognitive skills, Schunk and Ertmer [3] say that motivating factors like task interest and self-efficacy should also be taught in order to improve and help students use self-regulatory mechanisms. Young children's vocabulary development is aided by teachers' detailed explanations of the target word meanings during story readings [4]. Children engaged in word explanations through interactive education strategies that allow them to relate the word meanings to book pictures, story plots, and background information have significant short- and long-term effects on vocabulary learning. For language to be learned by inference rather than dictionary searches, learners must have experience in using this strategy. Therefore, word learning improves from interventions that provide students the opportunity to practice inferencing strategies. Interventions help learners get acquainted with inferencing techniques and have a positive effect on word learning. Another interesting study is using well-known songs promote the acquisition of new vocabulary in EFL learners, with "chanting" and "music videos with caption" techniques. This strategy developed an English vocabulary learning application using gamification and cloud intelligence approaches, using the prominent features of smartphones that provide learners with long-lasting incentive.

In Part III, the selected summaries present a reflection on the influence of Information and Communication Technologies (ICTs) on acts of learning and new ways of teaching. Research on the effects of three different types of electronic textual glosses, tooltip-type glossing, frame-type glossing, and concordance glossing, on foreign language vocabulary learning are studied along with a the third type that provides authentic concordance sentences for glossed words. Exposing learners to authentic concordance sentences, and comparing their effects with the two different formats of glossing is an interesting research summary followed by the effects of E-flashcards and paper flashcards on vocabulary learning and learner attitudes. E-flashcards (or digital flashcards).types of multimedia-assisted vocabulary learning materials, have been found to positively impact second language (L2) learners' word attainment [5, 6]. Perceived competence refers to student beliefs about their ability to do well in an academic environment (Ryan and Deci 36). Self-determination theory suggests that humans have innate needs for autonomy and perceived competence. Autonomous learning is seen as having control over what, when, where, and how students learn, as well as how their needs and interests are respected by teachers and other stakeholders [7]. Augmented reality (AR) is useful for supporting ubiquitous learning in authentic environments. It is a type of multimedia learning theory that creates a stronger connection between the digital content and the real environment. One of the studies focussed on the effects of multimedia annotations on incidental vocabulary learning and employing on-screen tests where visual elements are incorporated in hypermedia environments. Electronic and Paper Textual Glosses summary examined the effectiveness of electronic and paper textual glosses on second language vocabulary learning and reading comprehension within a cognitive load theory framework. The electronic glossing condition was also the most efficient in light of the cognitive load framework, showing the highest instructional efficiency. Self-directed learning on paper and mobile application flashcards is asstudy that explored vocabulary learning outcomes by using paper and mobile application flashcards. The study used a repeated measures design, by exposing the participants to different learning conditions. The findings underscore the long-term impacts of mobile-assisted vocabulary learning, and the affordances provided by such platforms for learning a considerable number of words by EFL learners. ESL Players' Use of Vocabulary Learning Strategies in Massively Multiplayer Online

Role-Playing Games (MMORPG) is an innovative study that investigated the impact of Massively Multiplayer Online Role-Playing Game (MMORPG) on players' application of vocabulary learning strategies. Apart from identifying the vocabulary learning strategies used by the ESL players during online gaming, in order to find out how aspects related to MMORPG influence the use of strategies. Using Gu and Johnson's [8] categorisation of vocabulary learning strategies (VLS), it was found that these ESL players utilise metacognitive, cognitive, memory and activation strategies in order to learn game-related vocabulary during the MMORPG gameplay sessions.

Review summaries for Part IV provide an introduction to corpora and terminology. As corpora may be implemented to improve learner language development and used as effective tools for improving vocabulary teaching and learning, corpora have a direct implications for classroom instruction. A new pedagogy called corpus-based language pedagogy (CBLP) is offered as a novel way to incorporate corpora into the classroom and support instructors' instruction as very few summaries convey fundamental ideas connected to corpora. Corpus linguistics and classroom pedagogy are combined in CBLP. To assist instructors in creating successful corpus-based lessons, four design elements are shown. Finally, a few significant concerns are brought forward to assist teachers in developing corpus-based lesson designs.

The first summary is about the KELLY project, and it includes work on developing monolingual and bilingual word lists for language learning, using corpus methods, for nine languages and 36 language pairs. It presents the approach to preparing the list for each language. Was as follows: Identify the corpus. Generate a frequency list (the 'Monolingual 1' or 'M1' list) Clean up the list, and compare it with lists from other corpora and other wordlists. Make adjustments to give the 'M2' list Translate each item into all the other KELLY languages (the 'Translation 1' or 'T1' list) Use the 'back translations' to identify items for addition or deletion. Make further adjustments to give the final M3 list. Another study focuses on using word lists where the vocabulary is checked for being common (frequent) versus rare (infrequent) in readability analysis where texts are analysed for their lexical frequency profiles. One perspective is about how linguistic and sociocognitive factors designate when, why, and how speakers say "sorry" and "I'm sorry" in two corpora of American spoken English, namely, the Michigan Corpus of Academic Spoken English (MICASE) and the Corpus of Contemporary American English (COCA) within pragmatic and socio-cognitive dimensions, hoping to bridge corpus linguistics and discourse analysis. Following Liu and Myers' approach (2020), one of the studies characterised the most common meaning senses of 150 PVs (a lexical verb and a particle) [9] among 500 TED talk transcripts based on corpus analyses and frequency information of meaning senses. Antconc, a computer program, was adopted to locate sentences in the TED Talks. A Study of Modal and Usage of Modal Verbs in the UCC (Uniform Commercial Code) and conducted a socio-semantic interpretation. An innovative study that highlights this section is combining intelligent machine algorithms with Japanese text sentiment classification. That provides a theoretical reference for subsequent natural language research. Through various comparative analyses, it shows that the research model has good comprehensive performance, meets the needs of the sentiment classification system, and can provide theoretical reference for related research. Lastly, one of the intriguing research that examines how gender is represented in EFL textbooks is Gender Construction in Teaching Materials by Combining Critical Discourse Analysis and Corpus Linguistics. The proof of a long-standing stereotype that domestic labour is seen as socially acceptable for women mirrors prior gender-based discourse studies [10]. The empirical evidence indicates that the textbook authors constructed gender stereotypes in terms of sports and reading.

Bibliography

1. Weinstein, C. E., & Mayer, R. E. (1986). The teaching of learning strategies. In M. C. Wittrock (Ed.), *Handbook of research on teaching* (pp. 315–327). Macmillan.
2. Schunk, D. H., & Ertmer, P. A. (2000). Self-regulation and academic learning: Self-efficacy enhancing interventions. In M. Boekaerts, P. R. Pintrich, & M. Zeidner (Eds.), *Handbook of self-regulation* (pp. 631–649). Academic. https://psycnet.apa.org/doi/10.1016/B978-012109890-2/50048-2" https://doi.org/10.1016/B978-012109890-2/50048-2
3. Zimmerman, B. J., & Risemberg, R. (1997). Self-regulatory dimensions of academic learning and motivation. In G. D. Phye (Ed.), *Handbook of academic learning: Construction of knowledge* (pp. 105–125). Academic.
4. Biemiller, A., & Boote, C. (2006). An effective method for building vocabulary in primary grades. *Journal of Educational Psychology, 98*, 44–62.
5. Başoğlu, E. B., & Akdemir, Ö. (2010). A comparison of undergraduate students' English vocabulary learning: Using mobile phones and flash cards. *The Turkish Online Journal of Educational Technology, 9*(3), 1–7.
6. Chuang, H. Y., & Ku, H. Y. (2011). The effect of computer-based multimedia instruction with Chinese character recognition. *Educational Media International, 48*, 27–41.
7. Reeve, J., & Jang, H. (2006). What teachers say and do to support students' autonomy during a learning activity. *Journal of Educational Psychology, 98*(1), 209.
8. Gu, Y., & Johnson, R. K. (1996). Vocabulary learning strategies and language learning outcomes. *Language Learning, 46*, 643–679.
9. Garnier, M. & Schmitt, N. (2015). The PHaVE List: A pedagogical list of PVs and their most frequent meaning senses. *Language Teaching Research, 19*(6), 645–666. https://doi.org/10.1177/1362168814559798.
10. Barton, A., & Sakwa, L. N. (2012). The representation of gender in English textbooks in Uganda. *Pedagogy, Culture & Society, 20*(2), 173–190. https://doi.org/10.1080/02188791.2014.924388

Chapter 2
Vocabulary and Acquisition

2.1 Machine Generated Summaries

Disclaimer: The summaries in this chapter were generated from Springer Nature publications using extractive AI auto-summarization: An extraction-based summarizer aims to identify the most important sentences of a text using an algorithm and uses those original sentences to create the auto-summary (unlike generative AI). As the constituted sentences are machine selected, they may not fully reflect the body of the work, so we strongly advise that the original content is read and cited. The auto generated summaries were curated by the editor to meet Springer Nature publication standards. To cite this content, please refer to the original papers.

Machine generated keywords: child, morphological, children, build, beck, carlisle, bilingual, young child, intervention, young, morphologically, biemiller, vocabulary instruction, growth, vocabulary word.

2.1.1 Self-Efficacy, Task Complexity and Task Performance: Exploring Interactions in Two Versions of Vocabulary Learning Tasks [94]

This is a machine-generated summary of:

Wu, Xiaoli; Lowyck, Joost; Sercu, Lies; Elen, Jan: Self-efficacy, task complexity and task performance: Exploring interactions in two versions of vocabulary learning tasks [94]

Published in: Learning Environments Research (2012)

Link to original: https://doi.org/10.1007/s10984-012-9098-2

Copyright of the summarized publication:

M. Udaya, C. R. Reddy (eds.), *Vocabulary, Corpus and Language Teaching*,
https://doi.org/10.1007/978-3-031-45986-3_2

If you want to cite the papers, please refer to the original.
For technical reasons we could not place the page where the original quote is coming from.

Abstract-Summary "The present study aimed for better understanding of the interactions between task complexity and students' self-efficacy beliefs and students' use of learning strategies, and finally their interacting effects on task performance."

"Results indicated a significant task effect for self-efficacy beliefs and task performance, and a significant interaction effect of sequence with task complexity for learners' self-efficacy beliefs in learning for both task versions, learners with higher self-efficacy beliefs had better task performances than learners with lower self-efficacy beliefs."

"The results also revealed a strong correlation between self-efficacy and the use of learning strategies for both tasks."

2.1.1.1 Introduction

"Taking into account the previous findings that students' self-efficacy beliefs are critical to academic achievement and instructional intervention [1–4], informed by the tenets of social cognitive theory of self-efficacy [5] and the cognitive mediational paradigm of instructional design [6–9], the present study investigated the interactions between task complexity and learners' self-efficacy beliefs, learners' self-efficacy beliefs and their use of learning strategies, and finally their interacting effects on task performance."

"In an effort to contribute to the insight into this research question, the present study examined the interaction between instructional tasks and learners' self-efficacy beliefs by manipulating the complexity of two language learning tasks."

"Tasks at different levels of complexity can affect learners' self-efficacy beliefs, as well as demanding different metacognitive and cognitive learning strategies."

"We were also interested to know whether tasks at different levels of complexity would be perceived by students differently, as indicated in the variable of learners' self-efficacy beliefs, and thus demand different use of meta-cognitive and cognitive learning strategies to perform the tasks."

2.1.1.2 Research Questions and Hypotheses

"In line with the review of literature above, we hypothesised that cognitively more-complex tasks challenge students' self-efficacy beliefs more because there are more elements (new declarative knowledge), namely, more new vocabulary items, to be dealt with in performing the task."

"Students' self-efficacy beliefs for simple and complex tasks are different depending on the specific version of the task that they perform."

"How do learners' self-efficacy beliefs about simple and complex versions of a reading and EFL vocabulary learning task affect learning outcomes?"

"We hypothesised that self-efficacy belief would be positively related to task performance on both tasks and that, at each task version, students with higher self-efficacy beliefs would perform better in the posttest following task execution."

2.1.1.3 Research Method and Procedure

"Both simple and complex tasks required the participants to attend to a reading passage (of about 281 words), and each of the target words in the same manner."

"Participants were also informed that, after they finished the task, their knowledge of the target words would be tested."

"Participants were asked to fill out the scale and indicate the frequency of using these strategies on learning the target words in the text from 1 (Never) to 7 (Always)."

"Participants were asked to complete both the task self-efficacy and vocabulary learning self-efficacy scales on this task."

"The sources of our data were: task complexity, self-efficacy scores from two scales, vocabulary post-tests and students' learning strategy measures."

"Results from the vocabulary pretest indicated that the target words were unfamiliar to the students participating in this study before the experiment."

2.1.1.4 Results

"These results indicate that the task complexity differentials led to the mean score differences in participants' task self-efficacy, vocabulary learning self-efficacy and task performance; however, results showed no significant task effect for the mean scores for learning strategies ($F (1, 70) = 0.01$, $p = 0.92$)."

"Further analyses revealed a significant interaction effect for task sequence with task complexity on learners' self-efficacy beliefs in vocabulary learning (Wilks' lambda = 0.94, $F (1, 70) = 4.78$, $p = 0.03$, $eta^2 = 0.06$ and observed power = 0.58)."

"With regard to the complex task version, ANOVA revealed similar significant overall effects for task self-efficacy ($F (2, 67) = 5.63$, $p = 0.005$, $ES = 0.14$) and vocabulary learning self-efficacy ($F (2, 64) = 10.83$, $p = 0.001$, $ES = 0.25$) on the use of learning strategies."

2.1.1.5 Discussion and Conclusion

"In line with the theoretical background of the study presented earlier in this article on task complexity and learners' self-efficacy beliefs, we were interested to know how differences in the cognitively-defined complexity of the tasks were reflected in learners' perceptions of their capabilities to perform on the task and learners' performance on the task."

"Further analysis of the change in self-efficacy beliefs for the two experimental groups at four measure points showed that the order in which simple and complex versions were performed had an interaction effect with task complexity for learners' ratings of their confidence in performing the tasks."

"The study examined the effects of increasing task complexity on learners' self-efficacy beliefs along a number of dimensions."

"Our results show that students' self-efficacy beliefs are significantly correlated to their use of cognitive learning strategies for both task versions, and vocabulary learning self-efficacy belief is positively related to task performance for the simple task."

2.1.2 The Crossover Effects of Morphological Awareness on Vocabulary Development Among Children in French Immersion [95]

This is a machine-generated summary of:

Lam, Katie; Chen, Xi: The crossover effects of morphological awareness on vocabulary development among children in French immersion [95]
Published in: Reading and Writing (2017)
Link to original: https://doi.org/10.1007/s11145-017-9809-2

If you want to cite the papers, please refer to the original.
For technical reasons we could not place the page where the original quote is coming from.

Abstract-Summary "The purpose of the current study was to explore longitudinally the bidirectional cross-language effects between morphological awareness and vocabulary development across English and French over 1 year."

"All were non-native speakers of French, and demonstrated average English word reading and vocabulary skills."

"The Grade 1 students were assessed in English only at pretest, and in English and French at post-test."

"The Grade 2 students were assessed in English and French at both time points."

"As predicted, regression analyses revealed that English inflectional awareness predicted unique variance in French vocabulary among Grade 1 students."

"Among Grade 2 students, cross-lagged analyses showed that both English inflectional and English derivational awareness predicted gains in French vocabulary between Grades 2 and 3."

"Counter to our expectations, French morphological awareness did not predict gains in English vocabulary over time."

2.1.2.1 Introduction

"The purpose of the present study was to explore longitudinally the bidirectional cross-language relations between morphological awareness and vocabulary among emergent English-French bilingual children."

"After more than two decades of research, there is now considerable evidence that morphological awareness contributes to within-language vocabulary learning in English (e.g., Carlisle [10]; Carlisle & Fleming [11]; Chen et al. [12]; Lam et al. [13]; McBride-Chang et al. [14]; Nagy et al. [15]; Sparks & Deacon [16]) and in French for both monolinguals and bilinguals (e.g., Colé et al. [17])."

"Research examining the cross-language effects of morphological awareness on vocabulary in English-French bilinguals is sparse, despite many shared morphological features between the two languages (described below) that may facilitate such transfer."

"Given the key role that vocabulary plays in reading comprehension (e.g., McKeown et al. [18]; Ouellette [19]), identifying cognitive processes involved in vocabulary growth leads to improved practices in vocabulary instruction, which ultimately can facilitate bilingual children's reading acquisition."

2.1.2.2 Development of Morphological Awareness

"Inflectional awareness and derivational awareness have been observed to transfer between English and Romance languages (e.g., French–English in Deacon and others [20]; Spanish–English in Ramírez and others [21, 22]), as well as between English and Semitic languages (e.g., Hebrew–English in Schiff & Calif [23]; Arabic–English in Saiegh-Haddad & Geva [24])—notably, all of these languages frequently use inflectional and derivational morphology in forming morphologically complex words."

"The majority of studies have focused on examining the transfer of morphological awareness to facilitate word reading across languages (e.g., Deacon et al. [20]; Ramírez et al. [21]; Schiff & Calif [23]; Saiegh-Haddad & Geva [24]; Chung & Ho [25])"

"Only a small number of studies have investigated cross-language relations between morphological awareness and vocabulary in bilingual children (e.g., Ramírez et al. [22]; Hipfner-Boucher et al. [26])"

"The present study was designed to investigate bidirectionally the cross-language relations between morphological awareness and vocabulary over 1 year by following a cohort of Grade 1 students and a cohort of Grade 2 students enrolled in an early French immersion program."

2.1.2.3 Method

"Only seven children in the younger cohort and four children in the older cohort were reported to speak English less than 25% of the time at home."

"For half of the items, the stimulus word was a stem/base and the children were required to produce an inflected/derived form of the stem/base word to complete the sentence."

"For the other half of the items, children were presented with an inflected/derived word and were asked to identify the stem/base to complete a sentence."

"The testing format was the same as the English morphological awareness tasks, in which children were asked to produce the inflected/derived form of a stem/base (e.g., Chanter: Ma soeur chante.) or the stem/base of an inflected/derived word to complete the sentences presented (e.g., Heureuse: Aujourd'hui, Paul a l'air très heureux)."

"Children were given three practice items prior to the testing items to ensure understanding of the task."

2.1.2.4 Results

"Final beta weights suggested that in addition to age and French word reading, both types of English morphological awareness measured at Time 1 were unique predictors of Time 2 French vocabulary."

"Follow-up analyses with interaction terms were carried out to determine whether the cross-language effects of English morphological awareness on French vocabulary differed by children's language status in the older cohort."

"To determine whether the cross-language effects of French morphological awareness on English vocabulary differed by children's language status (i.e., EL1 vs. ELL), follow-up analyses were performed with interaction terms [27]."

"None of the interaction terms contributed significantly to English vocabulary beyond the other predictors, thus indicating the effects of French morphological awareness on English vocabulary did not differ between the EL1 and ELL children in all the models."

2.1.2.5 Discussion

"By adopting a longitudinal design with substantive controls in the present study, we aimed to evaluate the cross-language associations between earlier morphological awareness and later vocabulary across English and French, while accounting for the maximum amount of spurious variance."

"The current pattern of results is consistent with the hypothesis that there would be significant cross-language associations between morphological awareness and vocabulary in English and French, beyond substantial controls."

"The association appears to be bidirectional: children's earlier English morphological awareness transferred to predict variance in later French vocabulary; at the same time, earlier French derivational awareness predicted significant variance in later English vocabulary among the older cohort."

"Results from the present study suggest that by the early elementary years, children had developed sufficient morphological awareness in English to apply this metalinguistic skill to their French vocabulary learning."

2.1.2.6 Conclusion

"This study demonstrated that among English-speaking children who are at the early stages in acquiring French as their additional language, English morphological awareness plays an important role in acquiring French vocabulary."

"Children who are better at manipulating morphemes and reflecting on morphological structures in English are also able to analyze and acquire novel French words more efficiently."

"Koda [28] has posited that in the initial stages of acquiring a second language, morphological awareness from the learner's first language is activated to serve as a filter through which one begins to analyze, organize, and understand input from the second language."

2.1.3 Word and Child Characteristics in Vocabulary Learning of Native English Speakers and Bilingual Learners [96]

This is a machine-generated summary of:

Zhang, Jie; Lo, Meng-Ting; Lin, Tzu-Jung: Word and child characteristics in vocabulary learning of native English speakers and bilingual learners [96]
Published in: Reading and Writing (2022)
Link to original: https://doi.org/10.1007/s11145-022-10293-3

If you want to cite the papers, please refer to the original.
For technical reasons we could not place the page where the original quote is coming from.

Abstract-Summary "This study investigated how word and child characteristics affect children's ability to learn the meanings of novel words."

"Students were taught the meanings of a series of novel words that were either morphologically related or unrelated."

"Results showed that compared to the EL group, the NE and FEP groups were better able to learn the meanings of morphologically related words than morphologically unrelated words."

"The effect of morphological relatedness on semantic learning was stronger for the target words with familiar suffixes than with novel suffixes."

2.1.3.1 Introduction

"The current study aims to investigate the extent to which word and child characteristics affect children's ability to use morphological cues (novel base words and existing suffixes) to learn the meanings of novel derived words (e.g., skaffist) and whether the relationships vary as a function of language status in native English speakers and bilingual learners with fluent English proficiency and designated English learners."

"We investigated a variety of child attributes including gender, grade level (fourth or fifth), language status (native English speakers-NE, fluent English proficient learners-FEP, designated English learners-EL), working memory, morphological awareness, word reading fluency, vocabulary, and reading comprehension."

"By taking both L1 and L2 status, and English proficiency level into account, Author studied three groups of fourth- and fifth-grade students: native English speakers, bilingual students with FEP and with EL, and found that the NE and FEP groups, with equivalent English proficiency, showed no difference but both groups were better able to use morphological analysis to infer new word meanings while reading sentences than the EL group."

2.1.3.2 The Present Study

"The current study investigated the word-level and child-level characteristics underlying a novel vocabulary learning paradigm that taps into the acquisition of lexical morphology, which emphasizes the understanding of roots of complex derived words [29], as well as derivation morphology that focuses on suffixes."

"The word-level attributes included morphological relatedness (related, e.g., blick/ blickable vs. unrelated, e.g., yord/ slomness), word type (familiar vs. novel suffixes), and morphological complexity (derived vs. root words)."

"Regarding the interaction effects between word and child characteristics, based on the literature, we hypothesized that students with higher English proficiency (NE and FEP) would be better than designated ELs at recognizing the morphological relations among the target words and using morphology to define novel morphologically complex words."

2.1.3.3 Method

"Participants were administered three individual tasks: novel word learning, sentence span, and backward digit naming, as well as other group measures: Extract the Base, Suffix Choice, Word Reading Fluency, vocabulary, and reading comprehension."

"Students completed a sentence by choosing an appropriate derivative given a base word."

"Of the 256 students included in the analysis, 194 (75.8%) had complete data, whereas 8 (3.1%) had missing data on at least one or more test trial outcomes of the word learning task."

"Bayesian cross-classified multilevel logistic models were fitted to examine students' responses (i.e., 1 = correct response, 0 = incorrect response) on the novel word learning task as a function of test trials, word-level, and child-level factors."

"The models included random-effect estimates, allowing the intercept to vary by child-level and word-level predictors and allowing the slope of test trials to vary by students."

2.1.3.4 Results

"The mean percentages of correct responses increased over time for all 12 items regardless of language status, indicating that students performed better over test trials."

"Three significant interaction effects were found: test trials and word type, language status and morphological relatedness, and word type and morphological relatedness, while other interaction effects were not significant."

"For students who learned the words with familiar suffixes, one test trial increase was corresponding to a 1.409 [exp (0.343)] increase in the log-odds of the probability of correct responses, which was higher than that of students who learned the words with novel suffixes [1.244 = exp. (0.218)]."

"For the words with familiar suffixes, morphologically relatedness was corresponding to a 1.422[exp(0.352)] increase in the log-odds of the probability of correct responses, which was higher than the novel suffixes condition [1.004 = exp. (0.004)]."

2.1.3.5 Discussion

"The significant interaction between English language status and morphological relatedness suggests that students with higher English proficiency (NE and FEP groups) were more capable than the designated ELs to use morphological cues among the target words to facilitate semantic learning."

"The current word learning task requires making explicit links between suffixes and lexical meanings, a more difficult and abstract level of morphological awareness [30]."

"The current word learning task, especially for the subset of words with novel suffixes, requires a more difficult and abstract level of morphological awareness than recognizing bases and suffixes, because it involves chunking complex words into meaningful parts and making links between suffixes and lexical meanings, which Wysocki and Jenkins [31] found challenging even for sixth and eighth-grade students."

2.1.4 *Effects of Morphological Instruction on Vocabulary Acquisition [97]*

This is a machine-generated summary of:

Bowers, Peter N.; Kirby, John R.: Effects of morphological instruction on vocabulary acquisition [97]
Published in: Reading and Writing (2009)
Link to original: https://doi.org/10.1007/s11145-009-9172-z

If you want to cite the papers, please refer to the original.
For technical reasons we could not place the page where the original quote is coming from.

Abstract-Summary "The effects of a 20-session intervention targeting morphological word structure on vocabulary knowledge were investigated in four Grade 4 and 5 classes, assigned randomly to treatment and control conditions."

"Hierarchical regression analyses controlling for initial vocabulary showed significant instructional effects on morphological analysis and vocabulary with words that were taught directly and novel words built on bases that were taught in the context of other derivations, but not for words with untaught bases."

2.1.4.1 Introduction

"Morphological instruction produced large immediate effects for deriving the meaning of morphologically decipherable instructed words compared to a comparison group who received vocabulary instruction about learning words from (non-morphological) context cues, and to a control group, but delayed effects were small."

"The morphological instruction in this study focused on 15 prefixes and five suffixes and how to use the meaning of these word parts in conjunction with root words (base words) to learn the meaning of new vocabulary words."

"Teaching students to discover spelling-meaning connections between words via a structured inquiry, problem-solving approach was intended to motivate children to see studying word structure as an interesting, engaging activity in accordance with researchers who encourage the development of "word consciousness" (e.g., Graves [32]; Nagy & Scott [33]; National Reading Panel [34])."

"This instruction used sets of morphologically related words to teach how to find meaning cues in consistent spelling patterns."

2.1.4.2 Method

"The scoring criteria were as follows: (1) two points were awarded for responses that showed a clear understanding of the target word, including base or stem and affixes, either by providing a definition, or by using the target word correctly in a sentence. (2) One point was given to responses that either (a) gave a vague sense of the meaning of the word by using it in a sentence, or (b) gave the meaning of one of the main morphemes (e.g., the produce or the re of reproduce), or (c) gave a vague sense of the meaning of one of the main morphemes by using it in a sentence. (3) Zero points were given if participants gave no response or if their answer was not connected to the meaning of target word."

"To demonstrate a gain from instruction on these words, students would have to apply knowledge of bases, affixes, and perhaps suffixing patterns to words that were not explicitly taught."

2.1.4.3 Results

"A 2 (group: experimental versus control) × 3 (Level of Transfer: near, medium, and far) ANCOVA was performed, with repeated measures on the second factor represented by the three types of words (Word Taught, Base Taught, and Affix Taught, respectively), for each of the outcome measures (Base Identification and Morphological Vocabulary)."

"For each level of transfer, the group effect was significant, for the near transfer measure, Word Taught, $F(1, 78) = 39.49$, $p < .001$, $\eta = 34$, for the mid transfer measure, Base Taught, $F(1, 78) = 28.02$, $p < .001$, $\eta = 26$, and for the far transfer measure Affix Taught, $F(1, 78) = 13.33$, $p < .001$, $\eta = 15$."

"The covariate was significant for each level of transfer: for the near transfer measure, Word Taught, $F(1, 79) = 35.6$, $p < .001$, $\eta = .31$; for the mid-transfer measure Base Taught, $F(1,79) = 20.2$, $p < .001$, $\eta = .20$, and for the far transfer measure Affix Taught, $F(1, 79) = 18.86$, $p < .001$, $\eta = .19$."

2.1.4.4 Discussion

"The first research question addressed whether students learn to identify the bases of morphologically complex words as a result of the instruction."

"Whether or not students received direct instruction about morphology, their ability to identify the base in complex words contributed a significant amount of variance to their knowledge of the words in the Morphological Vocabulary measure."

"This study provides evidence that a 20-lesson classroom intervention for Grade 4 and 5 students can teach morphological analysis knowledge and skills that provide them with a means to develop vocabulary beyond the words they are taught, but not beyond the morphological families that they are taught."

"The current study has shown that instruction about the details of written morphology aids the ability of students in Grades 4 and 5 to recognize meaning cues in complex words and build vocabulary."

2.1.5 Acquiring Foreign Language Vocabulary Through Meaningful Linguistic Context: Where Is the Limit to Vocabulary Learning? [98]

This is a machine-generated summary of:

de la Garza, Bernardo; Harris, Richard Jackson: Acquiring Foreign Language Vocabulary Through Meaningful Linguistic Context: Where is the Limit to Vocabulary Learning? [98]

Published in: Journal of Psycholinguistic Research (2016)
Link to original: https://doi.org/10.1007/s10936-016-9444-0

If you want to cite the papers, please refer to the original.

For technical reasons we could not place the page where the original quote is coming from.

Abstract-Summary "The present studies examined the effects of varying degrees of unfamiliar vocabulary within written discourse on individuals' abilities to use linguistic context for the purposes of translation and comprehension (i.e., lexical inferencing)."

"Results indicated that, as the number of foreign words per sentence, i.e., non-comprehensible input, increased the ability to successfully translate foreign words and create situational models for comprehension begins to decrease especially beyond five unfamiliar words per sentence."

"This result suggests that there is an optimal level of effectiveness in the use of a linguistic context strategy for learning foreign language vocabulary, but also that there is a limit to the strategy's effectiveness."

2.1.5.1 Introduction

"To better facilitate the vocabulary acquisition process, foreign language learners may frequently implement numerous techniques in the hope of acquiring the new vocabulary; yet, many leaners are quick to abandon a technique, or worse, leave attempting to learn a language altogether, potentially due to discouragement at what they see as substandard results."

"The common feature that exists between all vocabulary learning techniques is the hope that learners will be able to adequately acquire novel vocabulary."

"The context learning vocabulary learning technique (i.e., Lexical Inferencing) was evaluated for the purposes of acquiring foreign language vocabulary."

"The present studies attempted to estimate the degree (i.e., the point) at which vocabulary acquisition from linguistic context would begin to deteriorate; that is to say, where does attempting to acquiring novel vocabulary become too difficult for the novice learner when using a linguistic inferencing learning method?"

2.1.5.2 Learning Words in Context: Lexical Inferencing

"The use of linguistic context information and/or contextual cues for the identification of unfamiliar words in one's native language has been vastly explored; findings suggest that in instances when unfamiliar vocabulary appears, individuals are often able to accurately infer the meaning of the unknown word(s) based on the linguistic discourse cues which have been provided [35, 36]."

"For learning unfamiliar words in the reader's L1 (i.e., primary language) from written context, individuals with a low degree of knowledge of the unfamiliar vocabulary are able to use linguistic information (i.e., contextual cues) from written text as a means to increase their L1 vocabulary knowledge [35–42], a result which has been found for both children and adults [43–48]."

"Since language acquisition does not begin with higher level skills, it is critical to understand at what point foreign language learners are no longer able to use linguistic context strategies to acquire novel vocabulary."

2.1.5.3 The Input and Involvement Load Hypotheses

"For successful acquisition, the L2 input would need to be slightly above the learner's base level of knowledge (i.e., the task would not be found to be too difficult or too easy)."

"Applying these assumptions to the acquisition of the novel vocabulary, one can propose that a new language learner's i would approximate zero, since the individual is a novice learner who has had no exposure to the vocabulary being learned, and thus any exposure to that vocabulary would be above their i (i.e., above their current level of knowledge)."

"Based on these proposed assumptions for novel vocabulary acquisition, the current studies examined if novice learners would be able to adequately acquire novel vocabulary when utilizing a linguistic context vocabulary learning strategy, which varied the number of foreign content words per sentence based on substitutions made with Pseudo-Finnish or Spanish words."

2.1.5.4 The Present Research

"Using the predictions made by both models (Input and Involvement Load Hypotheses), Study 1 aimed to examine: (1) The utility of using a linguistic context strategy as the number of substituted content words increases from 0 to 3 novel words per sentence; (2) If substituting the number of primary content words, which were in the reader's native language (i.e., English), with 0–3 novel vocabulary words (i.e., items which were either Pseudo-Finnish or Spanish words) would impede the creation of situational models for comprehension."

"When comparing monolinguals and bilinguals on Pseudo-Finnish translations, however, Spanish–English bilinguals and English monolinguals scores should moderately increase from pre- to post-test, since there continues to be a large degree of contextual information that is known to those readers, although scores would at some point begin to decline as increasing L1 comprehensible contextual information is being lost due to the presence of more foreign words."

2.1.5.5 General Discussion

"The findings from this study are consistent with the findings from Nagy et al. [35] and Nagy et al. [36], who suggested that the use of the context learning method would allow individuals to successfully infer the meaning of unknown vocabulary in the learner's L1, based on the surrounding cues given by the text or speech."

"Even though this finding is of substantial interest, the most notable result stems from the findings in Study 2; even though individuals found the context learning method (i.e, lexical inferencing) to be useful for the identification of novel vocabulary, there was a limit to the usefulness of this technique."

"These findings provide support for Krashen's Input Hypothesis model in which it could be suggested that some of the basic properties of this model (e.g., degree of comprehensible input) may be useful when attempting to understand the method by which individuals are attempting to acquire information, either from a native or foreign language."

2.1.6 Improving the Acquisition of Novel Vocabulary Through the Use of Imagery Interventions [99]

This is a machine-generated summary of:

Cohen, Marisa T.; Johnson, Helen L.: Improving the Acquisition of Novel Vocabulary Through the Use of Imagery Interventions [99]
Published in: Early Childhood Education Journal (2010)
Link to original: https://doi.org/10.1007/s10643-010-0408-y

If you want to cite the papers, please refer to the original.
For technical reasons we could not place the page where the original quote is coming from.

Abstract-Summary "A total of 15 students were randomly assigned to three different intervention conditions: Word Only, which involves the simple verbal presentation of a vocabulary word; Dual Coding, in which a picture was paired with the vocabulary word, and Image Creation, in which students were told to create a mental picture of the vocabulary word in their mind and draw it on paper."

"A Latin square design was used, in which each group of students rotated through each of the interventions, being exposed to a different treatment condition for each category of words."

"While no statistical significance was shown between the interventions across the word categories, a significant difference was found between the Image Creation and Word Only interventions within the science terms category."

"Students also reported that the imagery interventions facilitated the ease with which they learned the words."

2.1.6.1 Overview

"Reading comprehension is a skill which requires a student to recognize words in text and understand their meanings."

"While there are a variety of methods for enhancing reading comprehension, text simply cannot be understood without knowledge of the words it contains."

"Vocabulary instruction helps students understand the meaning of words, and is crucial if students are to learn content from their school curricula."

2.1.6.2 Literature Review

"Vocabulary instruction and reading comprehension are intertwined."

"Enhancing the development and growth of the vocabularies of children enables them to better comprehend what they read, as struggling readers' comprehension improves with vocabulary instruction [49]."

"Cunningham and Stanovich [50] have shown that knowledge of vocabulary assessed in the first grade predicts over 30% of reading comprehension variance in the 11th grade."

"Vocabulary knowledge is a significant predictor of comprehension, as knowing the meaning of the words in a text is necessary for understanding it [51]."

"There are a variety of techniques based upon different theoretical accounts which can aid students in their development of word knowledge and reading comprehension, one of which is the dual coding theory."

"In one condition, students were instructed to create images to help them remember vocabulary words."

2.1.6.3 Present Study

"This preliminary study focused on three different interventions for presenting vocabulary to second grade learners: a Dual Coding method, in which an index card with a picture depicting the word was presented to the participants; an Image Creation method, in which the participants were told to create an image of the word in their heads and to draw the picture on paper; and Word Only, which involved the verbal presentation of a word."

"The interventions used in the present study increase the depth at which the vocabulary is processed, by adding an imaginal component, and linking the verbal code to the visual code."

"Using this framework, the Image Creation method would be the intervention which enables the vocabulary to be processed at the deepest level as the participant must become active in forming an image and drawing it on paper."

2.1.6.4 Hypotheses

"It was hypothesized that when students are instructed via imagery interventions, they would demonstrate better mastery of the vocabulary than when presented with only the word, because including both a verbal context and imagery creates a highly effective combination for learning vocabulary [52]."

"Students should demonstrate higher levels of vocabulary acquisition after the Dual Coding and Image Creation interventions compared with the Word Only intervention."

"The Image Creation presentation should be the second most effective intervention in aiding vocabulary learning."

"The least effective strategy for vocabulary learning would be the Word Only presentation, as the word is only presented in one code: verbal, and thus only allows for shallow processing."

2.1.6.5 Methodology

"Three different interventions were utilized in this study to manipulate the amount of imagery the students used when learning the vocabulary words: Dual Coding, Image Creation, and Word Only."

"Twenty-four hours following the instruction of each of the word categories, students were assessed as to their comprehension of the words taught by an experimenter designed vocabulary test."

"The researcher asked students in their groups to describe what methods they used when attempting to learn and remember the vocabulary words that were presented to them."

"Group B was trained using the Dual Coding presentation script, and was instructed on the meanings of the seven vocabulary words via this intervention method."

"On the second day of experimentation, which occurred 24 h after the initial instruction of words one to seven, students were tested on their vocabulary knowledge of this first septuplet of words using the experimenter designed vocabulary test."

2.1.6.6 Statistical Analyses

"To handle the missing data, the scores for the outcome measures of the students present in the group for that particular category and intervention were averaged."

"To test if group placement affected the results of the vocabulary outcome measures, a one-way ANOVA was carried out."

"To examine any effects due to the interventions the students used across the word categories, a repeated measures analysis was carried out."

"Data were separated by category of words, to examine if there were any interesting trends within each category, and an additional three-one-way ANOVAs were carried out."

2.1.6.7 Results

"There was no statistically significant difference between the interventions $F(2,24) = .170$, $p = .845$."

"It is interesting to note that the mean of the Dual Coding group was 4.00 words correct, which was higher than the Image Creation group ($M = 3.58$) and Word Only group ($M = 3.50$), but the difference was not statistically significant."

"The first one-way ANOVA examining the differences between the three interventions for the animals and habitats category did not demonstrate significant differences between them $F(2,12) = .894$, $p = .435$."

"The second one-way ANOVA, examining the differences between the three interventions within the musical instrument words, did not show a significant difference either $F(2,12) = .968$, $p = .408$."

"The third one-way ANOVA examining the differences between the three interventions within the science terms, demonstrated a significant difference $F(2,12) = 6.500$, $p = .012$."

2.1.6.8 Discussion

"Within the science terms category, the vocabulary outcome measure showed a significant difference between the Image Creation intervention participants and those in the Word Only intervention."

"Most of the students said that the interventions that used images, Image Creation and/or Dual Coding, had been the most helpful in aiding them with the memorization of the vocabulary words."

"It is interesting to note, that while the Image Creation intervention was significantly more effective than Word Only for the science terms, many students described the former method as being difficult."

"Many students mentioned that the Image Creation intervention would have been more helpful if they were allowed to keep the pictures they drew or were given examples of types of pictures they were supposed to draw."

"Students reported that the imagery interventions were more effective than the Word Only condition."

2.1.6.9 Concluding Remarks

"During the small group discussions students also reported that imagery facilitated the ease with which they remembered the vocabulary words."

"Even with these outside influences, the students reported learning a great deal and seemed to enjoy the exercises and strategies they were taught."

"The end result was also clear; vocabulary strategies involving imagery influence learning."

"Despite the type of intervention that is implemented, teachers must remember to stress the importance of vocabulary learning and reading comprehension strategies early on, both to further assist those who are doing well in continuing to learn and to bridge the achievement gap between students."

2.1.7 Phonological Decoding Enhances Orthographic Facilitation of Vocabulary Learning in First Graders [100]

This is a machine-generated summary of:

Chambrè, Susan J.; Ehri, Linnea C.; Ness, Molly: Phonological decoding enhances orthographic facilitation of vocabulary learning in first graders [100]
Published in: Reading and Writing (2019)
Link to original: https://doi.org/10.1007/s11145-019-09997-w

If you want to cite the papers, please refer to the original.
For technical reasons we could not place the page where the original quote is coming from.

Abstract-Summary "The purpose was to determine whether having students decode the spellings of vocabulary words improves word learning over passive exposure to spellings, and whether both treatments boost word memory compared to no spelling exposure."

"Students were taught the pronunciations and meanings of unfamiliar words over several test trials with feedback, one set with spellings present during learning but not when recall was tested, and one set with no spellings present."

"Results revealed that students remembered words better when spellings were seen than not seen during learning and on delayed posttests."

"Students who decoded spellings learned pronunciations and meanings better during the learning trials compared to students who only viewed spellings, but the advantage of decoding declined one and 7 days later."

"This was supported by a posttest showing that spellings were written more accurately when students had seen them than when they had not, with decoding producing better recall than exposure."

2.1.7.1 Introduction

"Studies of orthographic facilitation have examined not only whether learners remember pronunciations of vocabulary words better but also whether they learn meanings better when exposed to spellings."

"The current study extended previous studies by examining orthographic facilitation effects in low SES first-graders to determine whether having students decode the spellings of words would enhance memory for their pronunciations and meanings compared to exposure without decoding and compared to no exposure to spellings."

"The following research questions were addressed: 1. Will low SES first-graders learn the pronunciations and meanings of vocabulary words better when they hear and see the spellings of words during learning but not during testing compared to when they only hear but do not see spellings? 2. Will having students explicitly decode the spelling of words enhance vocabulary learning of pronunciations and meanings more than drawing no attention to the spellings? 3. Will orthographic facilitation of pronunciations and meanings still be evident 1-day and 1 week after the words have been learned?"

2.1.7.2 Methods

“Students were randomly assigned to one or the other of two vocabulary learning conditions in which they were exposed to spellings of six words.”

“Students in both conditions learned a second set of six vocabulary words without spellings following identical procedures.”

“For both sets of words, students were taught pronunciations and meanings during an initial study trial and during feedback periods on nine test trials.”

“In learning six words with spellings, students began with an initial study trial that preceded nine test trials.”

“Each word card was shown with its spelling printed beneath the picture, the tester pronounced the word and gave its definition, and students repeated the word.”

“To prompt memory for pronunciations, students were shown each picture of the words with no spellings present.”

“All students learned one set of vocabulary words with spellings and one set without spellings in a repeated measure design.”

2.1.7.3 Results

“To assess effects over trials, an ANOVA was conducted with treatment group, spelling exposure, and test trial as the independent variables, and recall of pronunciations as the dependent variable.”

“To assess effects on learning, an ANOVA was conducted with treatment group, spelling exposure, and test trial as the independent variables, and recall of definitions as the dependent variable.”

“Findings showed that both exposure to orthography and directing students’ attention to spellings through decoding helped students learn meanings as well as pronunciations of vocabulary words.”

“The absence of an effect of test point shows that students’ recall of pronunciations did not decline significantly from 1 day to 1 week, and the benefit of spelling exposure persisted.”

“Decoding skill contributed less because the experimenter gave feedback by telling students how to read the words, this may have compensated for any decoding skill deficiency and enabled weaker decoders to map spellings onto pronunciations in memory to support recall on the test trials.”

2.1.7.4 Discussion

“The addition of having students decode words may have provided extra practice that enhanced immediate memory for the learning events but did not strengthen the long-term bonding between spellings and pronunciations in memory.”

“Even though children cannot decode words, if someone tells them how to read the word, they can form at least a partial mapping between the spelling and pronunciation and hence store these connections in memory to advance their vocabulary learning."

"The current study suggests two procedures that hold promise of improving vocabulary learning: exposing students to the spellings of novel words along with their pronunciations and meanings; and enhancing students' attention to spellings by having them decode the words as they learn pronunciations and meanings."

"Findings from this study suggest that in addition to oral explanations and context examples, teachers might adopt the habit of having students view and decode novel words to connect spellings to pronunciations and meanings in memory."

2.1.7.5 Conclusion

"Present findings show that even children as young as first-grade can map spellings onto pronunciations to learn vocabulary words."

"The best way to insure that alphabetic foundational knowledge is acquired and that students learn to decode unfamiliar words is to implement systematic phonics instruction in the early grades [53, 54]."

"Decoding speeds up the learning of new words, both their pronunciations and meanings, compared to implicit exposure to spellings, and it better secures correct spellings of the words in memory."

"Results suggest the value of integrating spelling exposure and decoding into vocabulary instruction in order to improve students' learning of new words, especially students at risk for below-grade-level vocabulary knowledge."

"Results support connectionist theories of word learning, specifying that grapheme-phoneme connections are activated either through decoding or passive exposure and serve to secure spellings to pronunciations in memory and enhance the lexical quality of vocabulary words [55–57]."

2.1.8 Incidental Vocabulary Learning for Primary School Students: The Effects of L2 Caption Type and Word Exposure Frequency [101]

This is a machine-generated summary of:

Teng, Feng: Incidental vocabulary learning for primary school students: the effects of L2 caption type and word exposure frequency [101]
Published in: The Australian Educational Researcher (2018)
Link to original: https://doi.org/10.1007/s13384-018-0279-6

If you want to cite the papers, please refer to the original.

For technical reasons we could not place the page where the original quote is coming from.

Abstract-Summary "Research has emphasized classroom-based learning of vocabulary knowledge, with growing focus on the potential for using captioned videos and increased word encounters."

"The present study investigated the effects of various captioning conditions (i.e. full captioning, keyword captioning, and no captions), the number of word encounters (one and three), and the combinations of these two variables on incidental learning of new words while viewing a video."

"A total of 257 primary school students learning English as a second language (ESL) were divided into six groups and randomly assigned to a condition in which 15 target lexical items were included."

"A post-test, measuring the recognition of word form/meaning and recall of word meaning, was administered immediately after participants viewed the video."

"The combination of full captioning and three encounters was most effective for incidental learning of lexical items."

"This quasi-experimental study contributes to the literature by providing evidence which suggests that captioned videos coordinate two domains (i.e. auditory and visual components) and help ESL learners to obtain greater depth of word form processing, identify meaning by unpacking language chunks, and reinforce the form-meaning link."

2.1.8.1 Introduction

"Educators in Australia and worldwide have generally acknowledged the potential for using captioned videos to enhance primary school learners' vocabulary development, an important part of English language learning that carries long-term implications for future academic development."

"Online processing demands pose challenges to vocabulary learning through audio–visual input [58], exploring whether the various sources of information in captioned videos can be processed simultaneously for learners' incidental vocabulary learning is of interest."

"This limitation suggests a need to investigate the interplay between types of captions and word exposure frequency for incidental vocabulary learning."

"The combination of captioned videos and word exposure frequency may provide theoretical and practical possibilities to enhance incidental vocabulary learning in primary school students."

2.1.8.2 Literature Review

"Findings showed a positive effect of captions on the word form learning, but not on the learning of meaning for the Belgian English learners."

"Rodgers [59] proposed an average correlation ($r = 0.30$) between word exposure frequency and incidental vocabulary learning in a vocabulary test administered after viewing a captioned video."

"The present study will thus provide substantial insight into incidental vocabulary learning from captions, specifically by addressing the following questions: 1. To what extent does incidental learning of new words differ between three captioning types—full captioning, keyword captions, and no captions—when the three conditions include the same number of encounters with target words? 2. To what extent does incidental learning of new words differ between the two conditions involving different word occurrence frequencies (i.e. one and three) for each captioning type? 3. To what extent does incidental learning of new words differ between specific combinations of word exposure frequency and captioning conditions?"

2.1.8.3 Method

"Considering participants' vocabulary levels, the author assumed that learners would not struggle to comprehend videos with 95% of their words assessed at lower than the 2000-word level [60], allowing them to focus on extracting the meaning of the target words."

"Based on a pilot study involving a group of learners with similar proficiency levels and backgrounds, the 2000-word level was deemed suitable for participants in this study; the participating teachers also confirmed the suitability of this instrument."

"The first part measured receptive form recognition in which the learners were required to select "yes" if the target word appeared in the clip or "no" if it did not."

"All students were asked to watch the video and focus on its content without being aware of the main objective of the experiment (i.e. to assess the effect of captioning types and the frequency of word occurrences)."

2.1.8.4 Results

"The results showed a significant main effect of type of captioning on the three test parts [Wilk's lambda $F(3, 254) = 19.20$, $p < 0.05$, $\eta^2 = 0.08$]."

"The analysis also revealed a significant main effect of word exposure frequency on the three test parts [Wilk's lambda $F(3, 254) = 18.20$, $p < 0.05$, $\eta^2 = 0.07$]."

"A significant interaction effect was not detected between type of captioning and word exposure frequency [Wilk's lambda [$F(3, 254) = 18.26$, $p > 0.05$]."

"Irrespective of test types, learners who encountered words thrice in the full captioning condition significantly outperformed those who encountered words only once in the full captioning ($p < 0.05$), keyword captioning ($p < 0.05$), and no captions conditions ($p < 0.001$)."

2.1.8.5 Discussion

"Word exposure frequency appears to help learners focus on word form (i.e. pronunciation and spelling) along with the available cues in audio–visual input that can lead to meaning identification, encouraging more effective incidental vocabulary learning."

"Montero Perez et al. [61], learners recognized only 10.47 out of 18 (58.1%) word forms in the full captioning condition, but the effect of word exposure frequency on the full captioning condition further improved incidental word learning in the present study."

"Learners in the present study who encountered a word once could only recall the meaning of 4.57, 2.01, and 0.14 words out of 15 in the full captioning, keyword captioning, and no-captioning conditions, respectively."

"Providing different kinds of information through captioning possibly enhanced the students' incidental learning of word forms but overwhelmed their capacity to recall word meaning."

2.1.8.6 Concluding Remarks

"The findings of the present study indicate that primary school ESL learners can indeed learn new words by watching a video in English with full captions."

"When designing conditions for vocabulary learning in future studies, ESL teachers need to consider learners' varying trajectories in learning the different components of a word."

"Previous studies measuring the effects of captions on L2 learning used different types of videos, such as television reports [62], television programs [63], and documentary videos [64], whereas the present study solely used storytelling videos for young learners."

"Despite these limitations, the present study is the first to investigate different combinations of captioning types and word exposure frequency in ESL learning."

"A brief intervention combining three occurrences of target words encounters with a full-captioning condition resulted in positive incidental vocabulary learning among primary school ESL students."

2.1.9 Knowledge Building and Vocabulary Growth Over 2 Years, Grades 3 and 4 [102]

This is a machine-generated summary of:

Sun, Yanqing; Zhang, Jianwei; Scardamalia, Marlene: Knowledge building and vocabulary growth over 2 years, Grades 3 and 4 [102]
Published in: Instructional Science (2008)

Link to original: https://doi.org/10.1007/s11251-008-9082-5

If you want to cite the papers, please refer to the original.
For technical reasons we could not place the page where the original quote is coming from.

Abstract-Summary "Productive knowledge work and high-level literacy are essential for engagement in a Knowledge society."

"In the research reported in this article, students were engaged in sustained collaborative knowledge building in science and social studies."

"The vocabulary growth of 22 students over Grades 3 and 4 was traced, based on their entries to Knowledge Forum—a knowledge building environment used as an integral part of classroom work."

"High correlations between student engagement in knowledge building and vocabulary growth suggest that productive vocabulary can be developed through sustained knowledge building in subject areas."

2.1.9.1 Introduction

"In the present study, we used Lexical Frequency Profile to measure students' growth of productive written vocabulary in knowledge building discourse."

"Community knowledge building across curriculum areas provides an authentic context in which students can encounter, make sense of, and repeatedly use academic and domain-specific vocabulary in the service of the goal of idea advancement."

"The present study examines students' vocabulary growth, productive written words in particular, as a result of their sustained knowledge building in various curriculum areas over two school years: Grade 3 and then Grade 4."

"To provide a more detailed account of students' vocabulary use and growth in their knowledge building practice, this study further analyzes a specific inquiry conducted in Grade 4, focusing on student use of domain-specific terms in written discourse and their conceptual understanding."

2.1.9.2 Method

"The teacher helped integrate online and offline discourse by referring to Knowledge Forum notes during face-to-face discussions and encouraging students to record their questions, theories, and findings from face-to-face discourse in the database. (b) Collective responsibility for knowledge building and language use: Members in a knowledge building community share collective responsibility for communal knowledge advancement [65, 66]."

"When writing notes in Knowledge Forum, students were invited to elaborate their ideas and explain new terms so that others could understand their notes."

"In their four-month inquiry on optics in Grade 4, the students made 55 annotations in Knowledge Forum concerning language and rhetorical issues in peers' notes (e.g., "You missed the word…" "… does not make sense."

"Issues noticed in student writing in Knowledge Forum (e.g., spelling, word usage, grammar, writing organization) often became the focus of the Language Arts lessons."

2.1.9.3 Results

"In their Knowledge Forum notes, the students wrote about questions they were curious about, candidate explanations to be examined, related facts collected from experiments and observations, new information from reading material, responses to existing ideas as well as ways they were presented, improvements of thoughts, reflective syntheses of what they had understood and what they still needed to know, and inquiry plans to achieve their new goals."

"To examine the relationships between student participation in knowledge building discourse and their literacy performance, we analyzed the correlations between students' spelling, vocabulary, and reading scores and the percent of notes read and the total number of words written in online discourse over the two school years."

"The complexity level of students' ideas was significantly correlated with the number of total words (Pearson $r = 0.49$, $p < 0.05$) as well as the total occurrences of domain-specific words (Pearson $r = 0.54$, $p < 0.05$) and academic words (Pearson $r = 0.55$, $p < 0.01$) in students' notes written for the optical inquiry."

2.1.9.4 Discussion

"To examine the impact of extended, collaborative knowledge building on students' vocabulary growth, this study traced students' vocabulary use in online knowledge building discourse over two school years, and investigated the relationships between vocabulary use and the level of understanding achieved through inquiry."

"The extended knowledge building practice provides an effective means for enlarging students' vocabulary size, deepening their vocabulary knowledge, and bringing more words into productive use."

"The knowledge building practice brings about rich opportunities for developing students' academic vocabulary, which previous research suggests is hard to learn and use, and mainly developed through secondary and higher education [67]."

"The analyses of the word "opaque" and other terms in student writing suggested an incremental and interactive process of vocabulary learning through knowledge building."

"The idea-focused, progressive discourse brings students into contact with a variety of knowledge resources that involve new vocabulary use."

2.1.9.5 Conclusions

"This study investigated students' literacy engagement during their sustained, collaborative knowledge building in various subject areas."

"Student engagement in significant and sustained knowledge building was reflected in increasing numbers of notes written and read in Knowledge Forum."

"Students' use of general, domain-specific, and academic words were closely correlated to the level of understanding they achieved through knowledge building, as reflected in the qualitative evaluation of their portfolio notes."

"There were significant correlations between student engagement in knowledge building and literacy gains on the standard test."

"To better understand the complex picture of student literacy engagement in knowledge building, we will further examine vocabulary growth in relation to other literacy indicators such as syntactic complexity, writing organization, and dialogic contribution; and extend analyses to classes with more diverse student populations and greater literacy challenges."

2.1.10 The Effects of Science Instruction on Young Children's Vocabulary Learning: A Research Synthesis [103]

This is a machine-generated summary of:

Guo, Ying; Wang, Shanshan; Hall, Anna H.; Breit-Smith, Allison; Busch, Jamie: The Effects of Science Instruction on Young Children's Vocabulary Learning: A Research Synthesis [103]

Published in: Early Childhood Education Journal (2015)

Link to original: https://doi.org/10.1007/s10643-015-0721-6

If you want to cite the papers, please refer to the original.

For technical reasons we could not place the page where the original quote is coming from.

Abstract-Summary "This article synthesized science instruction studies with preschool and kindergarten children to understand the magnitude of science instruction's impact on young children's vocabulary outcomes."

"The overall mean effect size was moderate (0.66), suggesting that a focus on science increased young children's vocabulary outcomes."

"Educational implications of these findings suggest that there is support for using science instruction to increase the vocabulary performance of young children."

2.1.10.1 Introduction

"Compared with the other approaches to teach vocabulary (e.g., storybook reading), science instruction provides numerous ways for teachers to address both conceptual knowledge and vocabulary, such as mapping particular vocabulary onto children's mental representation about concepts [68, 69]."

"Science instruction can provide multiple contexts, including discussion, demonstration, hands-on activities (e.g., center activities), and informational or story book reading, in which children can learn and use new vocabulary."

"Typical approaches to teach vocabulary, such as storybook reading, primarily focus on improving children's knowledge of Tier 2 vocabulary words, rather than Tier 3 vocabulary words (e.g., Justice and others [70])."

"Science lessons can be hands-on science activities and/or informational book reading which may provide children with structured opportunities to apply their knowledge of the language that they were learning during the vocabulary instruction and internalize the science language [71]."

2.1.10.2 The Present Study

"The National Research Council (NRC) has developed A Framework for K-12 Science Instruction: Practices, Crosscutting Concepts, & Core Ideas [72] for teaching science content to school age children."

"Although current efforts are promising, there are limited science instruction studies in the early years and the full effects of science instruction on young children's vocabulary remain unknown."

"This article presents the findings of a synthesis conducted to determine the outcome of science instruction on vocabulary of children in preschool and kindergarten."

"The research question addressed is: What are the effects of science instruction in enhancing vocabulary outcomes for children in preschool and kindergarten?"

2.1.10.3 Method

"To be included in the present systematic review, studies had to meet the following criteria: (a) involve a training, intervention, or particular technique for teaching science in order to promote vocabulary learning for children; (b) include preschool and kindergarten aged children with no mental, physical, or sensory disabilities; (c) contain outcome variables that were standardized or researcher-developed measures of expressive and/or receptive vocabulary; (d) involve a (quasi-)experimental design that included a control group; (e) report sufficient statistical information to calculate effect size (e.g., means, standard deviations, t- and p-values); and (f) be reported in English."

"We excluded studies if the intervention did not include science component."

"Some studies were excluded because the intervention involved children with learning disabilities."

"We adapted Marulis and Neuman's [73] coding framework to code all relevant studies at three levels: (a) study characteristics, (b) intervention features, and (c) intervention outcomes."

2.1.10.4 Results

"To reporting the overall mean effect size, we also grouped studies by the two approaches to increasing young children's vocabulary through science instruction (i.e., science intervention including vocabulary instruction, vocabulary intervention with a focus on science) in order to facilitate the interpretations of the results."

"There were three studies that examined the effects of science interventions on young children's vocabulary learning [68, 69, 74]."

"Key components comprising the intervention included 32 science books (11 informational texts and 11 storybooks) and 14 social studies books (7 informational texts and 7 storybooks), 59 science and 35 social studies vocabulary words selected for instruction (all of which were Tier 2 and Tier 3 words), and explicit vocabulary instruction before, during, and after book reading."

"Results demonstrated that preschool children who received content-focused shared book reading intervention outperformed their peers who received "business as usual" shared book reading on the vocabulary outcomes with a medium effect size (0.40)."

2.1.10.5 Discussion

"This synthesis sought to determine the effects of science instruction in enhancing vocabulary outcomes for preschool and kindergarten children."

"Three science intervention studies showed a medium to large effect size and concentrated on increasing children's general receptive vocabulary [78] and domain-specific vocabulary [68, 69]."

"These findings are promising, because they suggest that young children can learn the complex vocabulary when shared book reading relates vocabulary to larger science concepts, provides multiple opportunities to interact with vocabulary, includes informational texts, and incorporates retelling and hands-on science activities."

"Two studies examined the effects of vocabulary intervention which includes multiple instructional components for vocabulary and incorporates the science follow-up lesson and showed small to large effect sizes [75, 76]."

"This synthesis provides preliminary evidence that science can be used to support vocabulary goals with children in preschool though kindergarten and recommends several instructional approaches to using science to teach vocabulary."

2.1.11 Supporting Young Children's Vocabulary Growth: The Challenges, the Benefits, and Evidence-Based Strategies [104]

This is a machine-generated summary of:

Jalongo, Mary Renck; Sobolak, Michelle J.: Supporting Young Children's Vocabulary Growth: The Challenges, the Benefits, and Evidence-Based Strategies [104]

Published in: Early Childhood Education Journal (2010)
Link to original: https://doi.org/10.1007/s10643-010-0433-x

If you want to cite the papers, please refer to the original.

For technical reasons we could not place the page where the original quote is coming from.

Abstract-Summary "The complexity of words makes vocabulary development a multi-faceted process that presents challenges to early childhood educators, offers benefits to young learners, and must be supported through evidence-based strategies."

"All students, regardless of socio-economic status or background, need to make significant gains in receptive and expressive vocabulary at home and at school each year in order to support their growth in literacy."

"The most effective way for early childhood educators to enhance the vocabulary development of all students is to implement evidence-based strategies for teaching vocabulary."

"In light of the trend in the research data that links the child's vocabulary level to gains in reading comprehension, early childhood educators have a special obligation to teach vocabulary more effectively."

2.1.11.1 Defining Vocabulary

"A highly educated adult has a listening/speaking vocabulary of about 10,000 words but likely knows nearly 10 times as many words in reading and writing, or about 100,000 words [77]."

"What may be less familiar—and particularly helpful—is the three-tier conceptualization of vocabulary [78]."

"Words that fit into Tier 1 include labels such as door, table, computer, and hippopotamus because these words are either already known or can be pictured, thus vocabulary instructional time is minimal."

"Tier 2 words have high utility for mature language users' listening, speaking, reading, and writing [78]."

"Vocabulary researchers agree that Tier 2 words should be the main focus when instructional time is limited [79, 80]."

"While these words will require some vocabulary instructional time within the content area, they are not worthy of extensive teaching time because they are not high-utility [78]."

2.1.11.2 Challenges in Acquiring the Concept of a Word

"Many of children's most charming language errors have to do with semantics, or word meaning."

"They sometimes turn to words they already know—for example, "vanilla" paper for "manilla" paper or "chickenpops" for "chickenpox."".

"Even when children apparently know a word, their understandings can be rather superficial."

"Multiple meaning words are often very challenging for young children."

"To really know a word's meaning is to know what a word represents and to begin to understand the network of concepts that goes with it [81]."

2.1.11.3 Benefits of Vocabulary Instruction

"Researchers have long acknowledged a relationship between vocabulary knowledge and reading comprehension [50, 82–85]."

"Students who begin school with more vocabulary knowledge tend to comprehend the texts they read and, as their reading comprehension increases, their vocabulary knowledge expands accordingly."

"Students who begin school with limited vocabulary knowledge may struggle with reading comprehension and that struggle will limit their vocabulary growth."

"Even in the very young years of a child's life, vocabulary instruction can influence that child's reading ability across the various subjects and throughout their school careers [80, 86–88]."

"Research suggests that there is the possibility of reducing the problem of low vocabulary knowledge and offers a wide array of research-based instructional techniques that can support all students in developing receptive and expressive vocabulary [89]."

"Possibly the most common method of vocabulary instruction in schools is to focus on words in the texts students read."

2.1.11.4 Research-Based Strategies to Support Vocabulary Growth

"In order for children to become proficient readers, they need to learn five to six new words per day, 38 words per week, 2000 new words a year, and 10,000 by age 6, vocabulary instruction is a must [77]."

"The prop boxes contain three to five storybooks, concrete objects that represent the vocabulary words the children will learn, a little book that contains pictures of the objects in the prop boxes, and a "Big Book" version of the same book [90]."

"In the Handbook of Reading Research (1991), there is discussion that students with high and low achievement show huge differences in vocabulary and that some differences are associated with socioeconomic level."

"It is important to consider what is causing the differences in vocabulary levels between children of lower and higher socioeconomic households."

2.1.11.5 Conclusion: An Agenda for Reform in Vocabulary Instruction

"Given the current research on differences in the vocabulary levels of students from varying socioeconomic levels and the critical role that vocabulary knowledge plays in reading comprehension, it is essential that early childhood educators make a concerted effort to build young children's storehouse of words."

"Utilizing dialogic reading, active involvement, and meaningful repetition of words should be a part of every classroom's vocabulary routine to ensure that all students make adequate vocabulary gains."

"As this research review has documented, high-quality vocabulary instruction is essential for all students but it is even more so for students who confront a wide variety of linguistic challenges [91]."

"Early childhood educators are charged with the responsibility of becoming familiar with the challenges that students from diverse backgrounds face in terms of improving vocabulary development and making every effort to ensure that all students make adequate vocabulary gains through the use of research-based instruction."

2.1.11.6 [Section 6]

"Each of these children has language strengths and areas for growth and each of them needs a teacher who understands vocabulary development and ways to support it."

"In the case of the 3-year-old twins, some misguided educators would assume that their language would develop effortlessly because they are economically advantaged when the research indicates that it is the language environment both at home and at school –particularly before third grade—that is the major influence [92, 93]."

"The research indicates that children from special populations need appropriate opportunities to learn new words and intensive instruction in vocabulary if they are expected to succeed [93]."

"The purpose of this article is to provide early childhood educators with the latest, research-based evidence on effective ways to build the vocabulary of young children."

Bibliography

1. Lorsbach, A. W., & Jinks, J. L. (1999). Self-efficacy theory and learning environment research. *Learning Environments Research, 2*, 157–167.
2. Pajares, F. (2002). Self-efficacy beliefs in academic contexts: An outline. Retrieved in September, 2004 from http://www.emory.edu/EDUCATION/mfp/efftalk.html .
3. Pajares, F., & Schunk, D. H. (2005). The self and academic motivation: Theory and research after the cognitive revolution. In J. M. Royer (Ed.), *The cognitive revolution in educational psychology* (pp. 165–198). Academic.
4. Zimmerman, B. J. (2000). Self-efficacy: An essential motive to learn. *Contemporary Educational Psychology, 25*, 82–91.
5. Bandura, A. (1986). *Social foundations of thought and action: A social cognitive theory*. Prentice Hall.
6. Duffy, T., Lowyck, J., & Jonassen, D. (1993). *Designing environments for constructive learning*. Springer.
7. Elen, J., & Lowyck, J. (1998). Students' views on the efficiency of instruction: An exploratory survey of the instructional metacognitive knowledge of university freshmen. *Higher Education, 36*, 231–252.
8. Elen, J., & Lowyck, J. (1999). Metacognitive instructional knowledge: Cognitive mediation and instructional design. *Journal of Structural Learning and Intelligent Systems, 13*, 145–169.
9. Lowyck, J., & Elen, J. (1994). *Student's instructional metacognition in learning environments (SIMILE)*. K.U. Leuven, Centre for Instructional Psychology and Technology.
10. Carlisle, J. F. (2000). Awareness of the structure and meaning of morphologically complex words: Impact on reading. *Reading and Writing, 12*, 169–190. https://doi.org/10.1023/A:1008131926604
11. Carlisle, J. F., & Fleming, J. (2003). Lexical processing of morphologically complex words in the elementary years. *Scientific Studies of Reading, 7*, 239–253. https://doi.org/10.1207/S1532799XSSR0703_3
12. Chen, X., Ramírez, G., Luo, Y. C., Geva, E., & Ku, Y.-M. (2012). Comparing vocabulary development in Spanish and Chinese-speaking ELLs: The effects of metalinguistic and sociocultural factors. *Reading and Writing, 25*, 1991–2020. https://doi.org/10.1007/s11145-011-9318-7
13. Lam, K., Chen, X., Geva, E., Luo, Y., & Hong, L. (2012). The role of morphological awareness in reading achievement among young Chinese-speaking English language learners: A longitudinal study. *Reading and Writing, 25*, 1847–1872. https://doi.org/10.1007/s11145-011-9329-4
14. McBride-Chang, C., Wagner, R. K., Muse, A., Chow, B. W., & Shu, H. (2005). The role of morphological awareness in children's vocabulary acquisition in English. *Applied PsychoLinguistics, 26*, 415–435. https://doi.org/10.1017/S014271640505023X
15. Nagy, W. E., Berninger, V. W., & Abbott, R. D. (2006). Contributions of morphology beyond phonology to literacy outcomes of upper elementary and middle-school students. *Journal of Educational Psychology, 98*, 134–147. https://doi.org/10.1037/0022-0663.98.1.134
16. Sparks, E., & Deacon, S. H. (2015). Morphological awareness and vocabulary acquisition: A longitudinal examination of their relationship in English-speaking children. *Applied PsychoLinguistics, 36*, 299–321. https://doi.org/10.1017/S0142716413000246
17. Colé, P., Royer, C., Leuwers, C., & Casalis, S. (2004). Les connaissances morphologiques dérivationnelles et l'apprentissage de la lecture chez l'apprenti-lecteur français du CP au CE2. *L'année Psychologique, 104*, 701–750. https://doi.org/10.3406/psy.2004.29686
18. McKeown, M. G., Beck, I. L., Omanson, R. C., & Perfetti, C. A. (1983). The effects of long-term vocabulary instruction on reading comprehension: A replication. *Journal of Literacy Research, 15*(1), 3–16.

19. Ouellette, G. P. (2006). What's meaning got to do with it: The role of vocabulary in word reading and reading comprehension. *Journal of Educational Psychology, 98*, 554–566. https://doi.org/10.1037/0022-0663.98.3.554
20. Deacon, S. H., Wade-Woolley, L., & Kirby, J. (2007). Cross-over: The role of morphological awareness in French immersion children's reading. *Developmental Psychology, 43*, 732–746. https://doi.org/10.1037/0012-1649.43.3.732
21. Ramírez, G., Chen, X., Geva, E., & Kiefer, H. (2010). Morphological awareness in Spanish-speaking English language learners: Within and cross-language effects on word reading. *Reading and Writing, 23*, 337–358. https://doi.org/10.1007/s11145-009-9203-9
22. Ramírez, G., Chen, X., & Pasquarella, A. (2013). Cross-linguistic transfer of morphological awareness in Spanish-speaking English language learners: The facilitating effect of cognate knowledge. *Topics in Language Disorders, 33*, 73–92. https://doi.org/10.1097/TLD.0b013e318280f55a
23. Schiff, R., & Calif, S. (2007). Role of phonological and morphological awareness in L2 oral word reading. *Language Learning, 57*, 271–298. https://doi.org/10.1111/j.1467-9922.2007.00409.x
24. Saiegh-Haddad, E., & Geva, E. (2008). Morphological awareness, phonological awareness, and reading in English–Arabic bilingual children. *Reading and Writing, 21*, 481–504. https://doi.org/10.1007/s11145-007-9074-x
25. Chung, K. K. H., & Ho, C. S.-H. (2010). Second language learning difficulties in Chinese children with dyslexia: What are the reading-related cognitive skills that contribute to English and Chinese word reading? *Journal of Learning Disabilities, 43*, 195–211. https://doi.org/10.1177/0022219409345018
26. Hipfner-Boucher, K., Lam, K., & Chen, X. (2014). The effects of bilingual education on the English language and literacy outcomes of Chinese-speaking children. *Written Language & Literacy, 17*, 116–138. https://doi.org/10.1075/wll.17.1.06hip
27. Pedhazur, E. J. (1997). *Multiple regressions in behavioral research: Explanation and prediction*. Harcourt Brace College Publishers.
28. Koda, K. (2007). Reading and language learning: Crosslinguistic constraints on second language reading development. *Language Learning, 57*(Supp. 1), 1–44. https://doi.org/10.1111/0023-8333.101997010-i1
29. McKeown, M. G. (2019). Effective vocabulary instruction fosters knowing words, using words, and understanding how words work. *Language Speech, and Hearing Services in Schools, 50*, 466–476.
30. Nagy, W. E., Diakidoy, I. N., & Anderson, R. C. (1993). The acquisition of morphology: Learning the contribution of suffixes to the meanings of derivatives. *Journal of Literacy Research, 25*, 155–170.
31. Wysocki, K., & Jenkins, J. R. (1987). Deriving word meanings through morphological generalization. *Reading Research Quarterly, 22*(1), 66–81.
32. Graves, M. F. (2006). *The vocabulary book: Learning and instruction*. Teachers College Press, Columbia University.
33. Nagy, W. E., & Scott, J. A. (2004). Developing word consciousness. In J. F. Baumann & E. J. Kame'Enui (Eds.), *Vocabulary instruction: Research to practice* (pp. 201–217). Guilford.
34. National Reading Panel. (2000). *Teaching children to read: An evidence-based assessment of the scientific literature on reading and its implications for reading instruction*. National Institute of Child Health and Human Development.
35. Nagy, W. E., Anderson, R. C., & Herman, P. A. (1987). Learning word meaning from context during normal reading. *American Educational Research Journal, 24*, 237–270.
36. Nagy, W. E., Herman, P. A., & Anderson, R. C. (1985). Learning words from context. *Reading Research Quarterly, 20*, 233–253.
37. Tabossi, P. (1988). Accessing lexical ambiguity in different types of sentential contexts. *Journal of Memory and Language, 27*, 324–340.

38. Moore, J. C., & Surber, J. R. (1992). Effects of context and keyword methods on second language vocabulary acquisition. *Contemporary Educational Psychology, 17*, 286–292.
39. Prince, P. (1996). Second language vocabulary learning: The role of context versus translations as a function of proficiency. *The Modern Language Journal, 80*, 478–493.
40. Rodriguez, M., & Sadoski, M. (2000). Effects of rote, context, keyword, and context/keyword methods on retention of vocabulary in EFL classrooms. *Language Learning, 50*, 385–412.
41. Webb, S. (2007a). The effects of repetition on vocabulary knowledge. *Applied Linguistics, 28*(1), 46–65.
42. Weber, S. (2007b). Learning word pairs and glossed sentences: The effects of a single context on vocabulary knowledge. *Language Teaching Research, 11*, 63–81.
43. Bolger, D. J., Balass, M., Landen, E., & Perfetti, C. A. (2008). Context variation and definitions in learning the meanings of words: An instance-based learning approach. *Discourse Processes, 45*(2), 122–159.
44. Brusnighan, S. M., & Folk, J. R. (2012). Combining contextual and morphemic cues is beneficial during incidental vocabulary acquisition: Semantic transparency in novel compound word processing. *Reading Research Quarterly, 47*(2), 172–190.
45. Cain, K. (2007). Deriving word meanings from context: Does explanation facilitate contextual analysis? *Journal of Research in Reading, 30*(4), 347–359.
46. Dockrell, J. E., Braisby, N., & Best, R. M. (2007). Children's acquisition of science terms: Simple exposure is insufficient. *Learning and Instruction, 17*(6), 577–594.
47. Gardner, D. (2007). Children's immediate understanding of vocabulary: Contexts and dictionary definitions. *Reading Psychology, 28*(4), 331–373.
48. Marinellie, S. A., & Kneile, L. A. (2012). Acquiring knowledge of derived nominals and derived adjectives in context. *Language, Speech, and Hearing Services in Schools, 43*(1), 53–65.
49. Rupley, W. H. (2005). Vocabulary knowledge: Its contribution to reading growth and development. *Reading & Writing Quarterly, 21*, 203–207.
50. Cunningham, A. E., & Stanovich, K. E. (1997). Early reading acquisition and its relation to reading experience and ability 10 years later. *Developmental Psychology, 33*, 934–945.
51. Braze, D., Tabor, W., Shankweiler, D. P., & Mencl, W. E. (2007). Speaking up for vocabulary: Reading skill differences in young adults. *Journal of Learning Disabilities, 40*, 226–243.
52. Sadoski, M. (2005). A dual coding view of vocabulary learning. *Reading & Writing Quarterly, 21*, 221–238.
53. National Reading Panel. (2000). *Report of the National Reading Panel: Teaching children to read: An evidence-based assessment of the scientific research literature on reading and its implications for reading instruction: Reports of the subgroups*. National Institute of Child Health and Human Development, National Institutes of Health.
54. National Early Literacy Panel. (2008). *Developing early literacy: A scientific synthesis of early literacy development and implications for intervention*. National Institute for Literacy.
55. Ehri, L. C. (2014). Orthographic mapping in the acquisition of sight word reading, spelling, memory, and vocabulary learning. *Scientific Studies of Reading, 18*(1), 5–21. https://doi.org/10.1080/10888438.2013.819356
56. Perfetti, C., & Hart, L. (2002). The lexical quality hypothesis. In L. Verhoeven, C. Elbro, & P. Reitsma (Eds.), *Precursors of functional literacy* (pp. 189–214). John Benjamins Publishing.
57. Share, D. (2008). Orthographic learning, phonological recoding, and self-teaching. *Advances in Child Development and Behavior, 36*, 31–82. https://doi.org/10.1016/S0065-2407(08)00002-5
58. Montero Perez, M., Peters, E., Clarebout, G., & Desmet, P. (2014). Effects of captioning on video comprehension and incidental vocabulary learning. *Language Learning & Technology, 18*, 118–141.

59. Rodgers, M. P. H. (2013). *English language learning through viewing television: An investigation of comprehension, incidental vocabulary acquisition, lexical coverage, attitudes, and captions* (Unpublished Ph.D. thesis). Victoria University of Wellington.
60. Nation, I. S. P., & Gu, P. Y. (2007). *Focus on vocabulary*. National Centre for English Language Teaching and Research.
61. Montero Perez, M. M., Peters, E., & Desmet, P. (2018). Vocabulary learning through viewing video: The effect of two enhancement techniques. *Computer Assisted Language Learning, 31*, 1–26.
62. Montero Perez, M. M., Peters, E., & Desmet, P. (2013). Is less more? Effectiveness and perceived usefulness of keyword and full captioned video for L2 listening comprehension. *ReCALL, 26*, 21–43.
63. Rodgers, M. P. H., & Webb, S. (2017). The effects of captions on EFL learners' comprehension of English-language television programs. *CALICO Journal, 34*, 20–38.
64. Markham, P. L., Peter, L. A., & McCarthy, T. J. (2001). The effects of native language vs. target language captions on foreign language students' DVD video comprehension. *Foreign Language Annals, 34*(5), 439–445.
65. Scardamalia, M. (2002). Collective cognitive responsibility for the advancement of knowledge. In B. Smith (Ed.), *Liberal education in a knowledge society* (pp. 67–98). Open Court.
66. Zhang, J., Scardamalia, M., Reeve, R., & Messina, R. (2009). Designs for collective cognitive responsibility in knowledge building communities. Journal of the Learning Sciences.
67. Corson, D. J. (1997). The learning and use of academic English words. *Language Learning, 47*, 671–718. https://doi.org/10.1111/0023-8333.00025
68. Henrichs, L. F., & Leseman, P. P. (2014). Early science instruction and academic language development can go hand in hand. The promising effects of a low-intensity teacher-focused intervention. *International Journal of Science Education, 36*(17), 2978–2995. https://doi.org/10.1080/09500693.2014.948944
69. Hong, S. Y., & Diamond, K. E. (2012). Two approaches to teaching young children science concepts, vocabulary, and scientific problem-solving skills. *Early Childhood Research Quarterly, 27*, 295–305. https://doi.org/10.1016/j.ecresq.2011.09.006
70. Justice, L. M., Meier, J., & Walpole, S. (2005). Learning new words from storybooks: An efficacy study with at-risk kindergartners. *Language, Speech, and Hearing Services in Schools, 36*(1), 17–32. https://doi.org/10.1044/0161-1461(2005/003)
71. Worth, K., & Grollman, S. (2003). *Worms, shadows, and whirlpools: Science in the early childhood classroom*. National Association for Education of Young Children.
72. National Research Council. (2012). *A framework for K-12 science education: Practices, crosscutting concepts, and core ideas. Committee on a conceptual framework for new K-12 science education standards, board on science education*. National Academies Press.
73. Marulis, L. M., & Neuman, S. B. (2010). The effects of vocabulary intervention on young children's word learning: A meta-analysis. *Review of Educational Research, 80*(3), 300–335. https://doi.org/10.3102/0034654310377087
74. French, L. (2004). Science as the center of a coherent, integrated early childhood curriculum. *Early Childhood Research Quarterly, 19*(1), 138–149. https://doi.org/10.1016/j.ecresq.2004.01.004
75. Neuman, S. B., Newman, E. H., & Dwyer, J. (2011). Educational effects of a vocabulary intervention on preschoolers' word knowledge and conceptual development: A cluster-randomized trial. *Reading Research Quarterly, 46*(3), 249–272. https://doi.org/10.1598/RRQ.46.3.3
76. Spycher, P. (2009). Learning academic language through science in two linguistically diverse kindergarten classes. *The Elementary School Journal, 109*(4), 359–379. https://doi.org/10.1086/593938
77. Byrnes, J. P., & Wasik, B. A. (2009). *Language and literacy development: What educators need to know*. Guilford.

78. Beck, I. L., McKeown, M. G., & Kucan, L. (2005). Choosing words to teach. In E. H. Hiebert & M. L. Kamil (Eds.), *Teaching and learning vocabulary*. Lawrence Erlbaum.
79. Nagy, W. E., & Scott, J. A. (2000). Vocabulary processes. In M. L. Kamil, P. B. Mosenthal, P. D. Pearson, & R. Barr (Eds.), *Handbook of reading research* (Vol. III, pp. 269–284). Lawrence Erlbaum.
80. Stahl, S. A., & Stahl, K. A. D. (2004). Word wizards all! In J. F. Baumann & E. J. Kame'enui (Eds.), *Vocabulary instruction: Research to practice* (pp. 59–80). Guilford Press.
81. Neuman, S., & Dwyer, J. (2009). Missing in action: Vocabulary instruction in Pre-K. *The Reading Teacher, 62*(5), 384–392.
82. Beck, I. L., Perfetti, C. A., & McKeown, M. G. (1982). Effects of long-term vocabulary instruction on lexical access and reading comprehension. *Journal of Educational Psychology, 74*, 506–521.
83. Coyne, M. D., Simmons, D. C., & Kame'enui, E. J. (2004a). Vocabulary instruction for young children at-risk of experiencing reading difficulties. In J. F. Baumann & E. J. Kame'enui (Eds.), *Vocabulary instruction: Research to practice* (pp. 41–58). Guilford Press.
84. Hiebert, E. H., & Kamil, M. L. (2005). *Teaching and learning vocabulary: Bringing research to practice*. Lawrence Erlbaum.
85. Stahl, S. A., & Nagy, W. E. (2006). *Teaching word meanings*. Lawrence Erlbaum.
86. Biemiller, A. (2004). Teaching vocabulary in the primary grades. In J. F. Baumann & E. J. Kame'enui (Eds.), *Vocabulary instruction: Research to practice* (pp. 28–40). Guilford Press.
87. Hargrave, A. C., & Senechal, M. (2000). A book reading intervention with preschool children who have limited vocabularies: The benefits of regular reading and dialogic reading. *Early Childhood Research Quarterly, 15*(1), 75–90.
88. Juel, C., Biancarosa, G., Coker, D., & Deffes, R. (2003). Walking with Rosie: A cautionary tale of early reading instruction. *Educational Leadership, 60*(7), 12–18.
89. Christ, T., & Wang, X. C. (2010). Bridging the vocabulary gap: What the research tells us about vocabulary instruction in early childhood. *Young Children, 65*(4), 83–91.
90. Wasik, B., Karweit, N., Bond, M., Burns Woodruff, L., Jaeger, G., & Adee, S. (2000). Early learning in CRESPAR. *Journal of Education for Students Placed at Risk, 5*(1/2), 93–107.
91. Hemphill, L., & Tivnan, T. (2008). The importance of early vocabulary for literacy achievement in high-poverty schools. *Journal of Education for Students Placed at Risk, 13*(4), 426–451.
92. Biemiller, A. (2003). Vocabulary: Needed if more children are to read well. *Reading Psychology, 24*(3/4), 323–335.
93. Wasik, B., Bond, M., & Hindman, A. (2006). The effects of a language and literacy intervention on head start children and teachers. *Journal of Educational Psychology, 98*(1), 63–74.
94. Wu, X., Lowyck, J., Sercu, L., & Elen, J. (2012). Jan self-efficacy, task complexity and task performance: Exploring interactions in two versions of vocabulary learning tasks. *Learning Environments Research, 15*, 17–35. https://doi.org/10.1007/s10984-012-9098-2
95. Lam, K., & Chen, X. (2017). The crossover effects of morphological awareness on vocabulary development among children in French immersion. *Reading and Writing, 31*, 1893–1921. https://doi.org/10.1007/s11145-017-9809-2
96. Zhang, J., Lo, M.-T., & Lin, T.-J. (2022). Word and child characteristics in vocabulary learning of native English speakers and bilingual learners. *Reading and Writing, 36*, 147–173. https://doi.org/10.1007/s11145-022-10293-3
97. Bowers, P. N., & Kirby, J. R. (2009). Effects of morphological instruction on vocabulary acquisition. *Reading and Writing, 23*, 515–537. https://doi.org/10.1007/s11145-009-9172-z
98. de la Garza, B., & Harris, R. J. (2016). Acquiring foreign language vocabulary through meaningful linguistic context: Where is the limit to vocabulary learning? *Journal of Psycholinguistic Research, 46*, 395–413. https://doi.org/10.1007/s10936-016-9444-0

99. Cohen, M. T., & Johnson, H. L. (2010). Improving the Acquisition of Novel Vocabulary through the use of imagery interventions. *Early Childhood Education Journal, 38*, 357–366. https://doi.org/10.1007/s10643-010-0408-y
100. Chambrè, S. J., Ehri, L. C., & Ness, M. (2019). Phonological decoding enhances orthographic facilitation of vocabulary learning in first graders. *Reading and Writing, 33*, 1133–1162. https://doi.org/10.1007/s11145-019-09997-w
101. Teng, F. (2018). Incidental vocabulary learning for primary school students: The effects of L2 caption type and word exposure frequency. *The Australian Educational Researcher, 46*, 113–136. https://doi.org/10.1007/s13384-018-0279-6
102. Sun, Y., Zhang, J., & Scardamalia, M. (2008). Knowledge building and vocabulary growth over two years, grades 3 and 4. *Instructional Science, 38*, 147–171. https://doi.org/10.1007/s11251-008-9082-5
103. Guo, Y., Wang, S., Hall, A. H., Breit-Smith, A., & Busch, J. (2015). The effects of science instruction on young children's vocabulary learning: A research synthesis. *Early Childhood Education Journal, 44*, 359–367. https://doi.org/10.1007/s10643-015-0721-6
104. Jalongo, M., & Renck; Sobolak, Michelle J. (2010). Supporting young children's vocabulary growth: The challenges, the benefits, and evidence-based strategies. *Early Childhood Education Journal, 38*, 421–429. https://doi.org/10.1007/s10643-010-0433-x

Chapter 3
Vocabulary Teaching and Learning Strategies

3.1 Machine Generated Summaries

Disclaimer: The summaries in this chapter were generated from Springer Nature publications using extractive AI auto-summarization: An extraction-based summarizer aims to identify the most important sentences of a text using an algorithm and uses those original sentences to create the auto-summary (unlike generative AI). As the constituted sentences are machine selected, they may not fully reflect the body of the work, so we strongly advise that the original content is read and cited. The auto generated summaries were curated by the editor to meet Springer Nature publication standards. To cite this content, please refer to the original papers.

Machine generated keywords: inference, lexical inference, user, strategy, efl, learn strategy, vl, target word, selfefficacy, technique, experimental group, lexical, system, experimental, question.

3.1.1 Collaborative Filtering for Expansion of Learner's Background Knowledge in Online Language Learning: Does "Top-Down" Processing Improve Vocabulary Proficiency? [73]

This is a machine-generated summary of:

Yamada, Masanori; Kitamura, Satoshi; Matsukawa, Hideya; Misono, Tadashi; Kitani, Noriko; Yamauchi, Yuhei: Collaborative filtering for expansion of learner's background knowledge in online language learning: does "top-down" processing improve vocabulary proficiency? [73]
Published in: Educational technology research and development (2014)

M. Udaya, C. R. Reddy (eds.), *Vocabulary, Corpus and Language Teaching*,
https://doi.org/10.1007/978-3-031-45986-3_3

Link to original: https://doi.org/10.1007/s11423-014-9344-7

If you want to cite the papers, please refer to the original.
For technical reasons we could not place the page where the original quote is coming from.

Abstract-Summary "This study aims to develop and evaluate an online English vocabulary learning system using collaborative filtering that allows learners to learn English vocabulary while expanding their interests."

"The online learning environment recommends English news articles using information obtained from other users with similar interests."

"The learner then studies these recommended articles as a method of learning English."

3.1.1.1 Introduction

"As the amount of information available on the Internet is increasing at a tremendous rate, recommendation algorithms have become important tools for users seeking to retrieve focused information, and have thus been applied to various online services."

"A recommendation algorithm is one that predicts a user's attributions, such as ability and preference, and suggests information that corresponds with these data."

"Collaborative filtering is a recommendation algorithm that predicts an active user's preferences and presents suggested material by using the preferences of users who appear similar to the active user according to their rating data."

"By previous research (e.g., Herlocker et al. [1]; Resnick et al. [2]), recommendation algorithms aim to determine a user's preferences and suggest optimized information according to that determination."

3.1.1.2 Related Works

"Collaborative filtering works to optimize an exact fit with learners' preferences and interests; thus, it supports top-down processing for comprehension in foreign language learning."

"This study aims to develop and evaluate the effect of a foreign language learning support system that uses a collaborative filtering system to recommend news articles that are close to, rather than an exact fit with, learner preferences, in order to expand background knowledge to promote top-down processing."

"This study aims to develop and evaluate an English vocabulary learning support system with collaborative filtering that recommends English news articles on topics that are close to learners' preferences and interests, and to compare this system with the popular earlier collaborative filtering algorithm known as "GroupLens" [2]."

"This research aims to investigate the effects of the new collaborative filtering algorithm, which recommends English news article in which learners have some interest (not strong interest), on perceived appropriateness of recommendation and learning performance."

3.1.1.3 System

"On the server side, five functions are implicated: user certification, news articles distribution, collaborative filtering, a user log function that collects what functions learners used and when, and a news scraping that regularly collects news article data from a news article company's website."

"The news article recommendation function displays on the main screen a list of articles that are based on the learner's interests."

"2: The system makes data set "Y_{ai}" of news articles that are rated positively by both active user a and user i. 3: The system evaluates the similarity of interest in news articles between users a and i, according to the rank correlation coefficient ρ_{ai} using the rating data from new articles including dataset Y_{ai} Herlocker et al. [1] reported that Spearman's rank correlation coefficient was a higher threshold resulting in an accurate fit rate, thus improving the GroupLens algorithm."

3.1.1.4 Experiment

"The group that studied English news articles recommended by the user-based collaborative filtering algorithm developed for this study will be called the experimental group, and the group that studied English news articles recommended by the basic user-based collaborative filtering algorithm will be called the control group."

"There were no differences between the control and experiment groups in terms of the function of the system except for the collaborative filtering algorithm."

"For 1 month, the experimental group studied from recommendations made with the user-based collaborative filtering algorithm developed in this study, while the control group continued with recommendations made by the algorithm of Resnick et al. [2]."

"During this time, learners completed a post-questionnaire and took an 80-item English vocabulary test based on JACET 8000; this was the same test they took before the experiment began."

3.1.1.5 Results

"We examined the difference in number of dropped-out learners between the experimental and control groups, including the subjects who had a pre-test score of over 50."

"The comparison of the average number of rated articles by category also showed no significant difference between the experimental and control groups."

"As the t-test results for the total and each category's numbers for learners' interest ratings in the news articles show, we did not confirm a significant difference between the experiment and control groups."

"These results show that the experimental group had overall higher scores in the English vocabulary test category when compared to the control group."

"d = .17), the average scores on the JACET 8000 English vocabulary post-test showed a significant difference (the experimental group: Mean = 43.83, SD = 9.35; the control group: Mean = 40.07, SD = 8.85; $t(96.87) = 2.04$, $p < .05$, $d = .41$)."

3.1.1.6 Discussion

"The researchers hypothesized that receiving recommendations from the collaborative filtering algorithm developed in this study allows learners to read a wide range of English news articles and possibly leads to higher learning results."

"In order to explain the effects of the collaborative filtering algorithm developed in this study, we posed four research questions: (1) Is there a difference in the fit rate of recommendation between the collaborative filtering developed in this research and GroupLens? (2) Does this collaborative filtering promote diversity in topics of news articles? (3) Does the system tend to recommend specific topics in order to promote specific vocabulary acquisition? (4) Overall, does this system contribute to the improvement of vocabulary test scores?"

"These results indicate that the collaborative filtering developed in this study contributes to the enhancement of vocabulary proficiency with the support of "top-down" processing [3] through learning with news articles closely related to the learners' interests."

3.1.1.7 Conclusion

"This study aims to examine the effect of collaborative filtering that predicts the degree of learner interest in unread English news articles and compare it to that of general collaborative filtering, which aims to predict the accurate fit rate of learner interest."

"The results of this research reveal that the system developed in this study allowed learners to read various genres of English news articles and to improve their vocabulary proficiency even though there was no difference between the collaborative filtering developed in this study and the general filtering system in the perceived fit rate of recommendations, despite the difference in the simulation test between the algorithm developed in this study and GroupLens."

"We focused on vocabulary proficiency levels, although using other parameters concerning learners' proficiency levels such as the length of news articles could also improve the perceived fit rate in terms of learners' proficiency levels."

3.1.2 *The Comparative Effects of Teacher Versus Peer-Scaffolding on EFL Learners' Incidental Vocabulary Learning and Reading Comprehension: A Socio-Cultural Perspective [74]*

This is a machine-generated summary of:

Jamali Kivi, Parivash; Namaziandost, Ehsan; Fakhri Alamdari, Ebrahim; Ryafikovna Saenko, Natalya; Inga-Arias, Miguel; Fuster-Guillén, Doris; Sirisakpanich, Dusita; Nasirin, Chairun: The Comparative Effects of Teacher Versus Peer-Scaffolding on EFL Learners' Incidental Vocabulary Learning and Reading Comprehension: A Socio-Cultural Perspective [74]

Published in: Journal of Psycholinguistic Research (2021)

Link to original: https://doi.org/10.1007/s10936-021-09800-4

If you want to cite the papers, please refer to the original.

For technical reasons we could not place the page where the original quote is coming from.

Abstract-Summary "Drawing on sociocultural theory, and multiple empirical studies conducted on the effectiveness of scaffolding on second or foreign language learning, the authors investigated the application of various forms of scaffolding (i.e., teacher versus peer-scaffolding) on EFL learners' incidental vocabulary learning and reading comprehension performance through a sociocultural perspective."

"The vocabulary and reading comprehension pre-tests were administered to the three groups."

"The vocabulary and reading comprehension post-tests were administered."

"The results showed that both experimental groups had better performance than the control group and there was a significant difference between teacher-scaffolding and peer-scaffolding in both vocabulary knowledge and reading comprehension performance and the peer-scaffolding group had a better performance than the teacher-scaffolding group."

3.1.2.1 Introduction

"Despite the existence of numerous scaffolding strategies in this field, very little research has been done to the best of the researcher's knowledge to investigate the comparative effectiveness of question answering and question generating to reveal the privilege of one strategy over another to improve EFL learners' reading comprehension."

"The effects of various scaffoldings of peer and teacher, such as skimming, scanning, warm-up activities, L1 translation, and their effects on the reading comprehension development and incidental vocabulary learning of EFL students need to be investigated."

"Considering the above-mentioned issues, this study aimed to investigate the comparative impacts of teacher and peer scaffolding on EFL learners' incidental vocabulary learning and reading comprehension through a sociocultural perspective."

"Two research questions were formulated: RQ1: Does applying teacher and peer scaffolding have any significant effects on Iranian pre-intermediate EFL learners' incidental vocabulary learning?"

3.1.2.2 Review of the Related Literature

"In a study, Jafari [4] investigated the effectiveness of scaffolding on Iranian EFL language learners' vocabulary knowledge."

"Khajeh Khosravi [5] attempted to find out the effect of symmetrical scaffolding on advanced learners' reading comprehension."

"The findings revealed that symmetrical scaffolding had a significant impact on EFL learners' reading comprehension performance."

"Talebinejad and Akhgar [6] investigated the effects of teacher scaffolding on Iranian EFL learners' listening comprehension."

"Carried out by Izanlu and Feyli [7], they investigated the extent to which two approaches to scaffolding, namely the Symmetrical and Asymmetrical, contribute to grammar acquisition among Iranian EFL university students."

"The data analysis indicated that AS scaffolding was a more effective strategy in improving EFL learners' grammar achievement."

"This study was run to check the impact of teacher versus peer scaffolding on EFL learners' incidental vocabulary learning and reading comprehension through a sociocultural viewpoint."

3.1.2.3 Methodology

"60 out of 80 EFL learners studying English at private Language Institute in Amol, Mazandaran Province were selected through administrating an Oxford Placement Test (OPT)."

"The teacher-made vocabulary test was pilot tested on a similar sample of learners from a different language institute."

"Before carrying out the study, a pilot study to examine the reliability of the vocabulary and reading tests."

"This study Through administrating an OPT to 80 EFL learners studying English at a private Language Institute in Amol, Mazandaran, 60 participants who scored ±1 standard deviation above and below the mean was selected as the sample of the study and divided into three groups: two experimental groups: GROUP 1: Teacher-scaffolding group (N = 20); GROUP 2: Peer-scaffolding group (N = 20); GROUP 3: Control group (N = 20)."

"The vocabulary and reading comprehension tests as the pretests were administered to all three groups."

3.1.2.4 Results

"The first research question aimed to find out whether teacher and peer scaffolding have any significant effects on Iranian pre-intermediate EFL learners' incidental vocabulary learning or not."

"Table 7 shows the differences among three groups (Teacher-scaffolding, Peer-scaffolding, and the control groups)."

"There was a significant difference between Teacher-scaffolding, Peer-scaffolding, and the control group in vocabulary learning."

"There was a significant difference between the teacher-scaffolding group and the control group."

"There was a significant difference between Teacher-scaffolding, Peer-scaffolding, and the control group in reading comprehension performance."

"The findings showed that peer scaffolding outperformed both teacher-scaffolding and control groups significantly."

"There was a significant difference between the teacher-scaffolding group and the control group."

3.1.2.5 Discussion

"The main purpose of the present study was to compare the effects of teacher versus peer scaffolding on EFL learners' incidental vocabulary learning and reading comprehension through a socio-cultural perspective."

"The results related to the first research question revealed that there was a significant difference among teacher-scaffolding, peer-scaffolding, and control groups regarding the vocabulary scores."

"The results dealing with the second research question showed that there was a significant difference among the teacher-scaffolding, peer-scaffolding, and control groups considering learners' reading comprehension scores in favor of the peer-scaffolding group."

"To improve learners' cognitive abilities, scaffolding instruction in the context of classroom learning and student research delivers efficiency."

"From a sociocultural perspective as used in the present study, both the teacher and peers have shown to be influential in applying a variety of scaffolding behaviors to help the students learn vocabulary and enhance reading comprehension to reach higher states of independence."

3.1.2.6 Conclusion

"It is more challenging when it comes to EFL learners with restricted exposure to language and the opportunity to use learned words in genuine contexts."

"The number of research studies carried out on finding the most effective vocabulary learning strategies is evidence of the effective role of strategies in word acquisition [8]."

"Since the current study focused on EFL learners' incidental vocabulary learning and reading comprehension, the obtained result may have been affected by the reading behavior of learners' L1 reading."

"The findings of the present study recommend applying more social and cooperative techniques in language learning and teaching context."

"Relying on the outcomes of this study, instructors are advised to use scaffolding to teach vocabulary in a technology-enhanced setting as an efficient substitute for traditional training."

"Upcoming studies can extend the experiment time and examine the effects of peer and teacher scaffoldings on different skills and subskills in different contexts."

3.1.3 Promoting Self-Regulation in Vocabulary Learning Among Chinese EFL Learners: A Needs Analysis [75]

This is a machine-generated summary of:

Ping, Aminah Ma; Baranovich, Diana-Lea; Manueli, Maria Khristina; Siraj, Saedah: Promoting Self-Regulation in Vocabulary Learning among Chinese EFL Learners: A Needs Analysis [75]

Published in: The Asia-Pacific Education Researcher (2014)
Link to original: https://doi.org/10.1007/s40299-013-0166-x

If you want to cite the papers, please refer to the original.

For technical reasons we could not place the page where the original quote is coming from.

Abstract-Summary "Learning strategies and motivational beliefs (e.g., self-efficacy) are the key, interrelated factors of self-regulated learning, which are crucial for learners' academic performance."

"This study investigated Chinese English Foreign language (EFL) learners' needs in terms of cognitive and metacognitive strategy use, as well as their perceptions and knowledge in vocabulary learning."

"It also indicated that learners' low self-efficacy and motivation might be due to the lack of strategy knowledge, which in turn affects their strategy performance."

"The study suggests that there is a pressing need to enhance learners' self-regulation in learning vocabulary through explicit strategy instruction, which emphasizes cognitive, metacognitive, and motivational aspects of learning."

3.1.3.1 Introduction

"Along with this domain of research, self-regulated learning (SRL), a multidimensional construct that involves cognitive, metacognitive, motivational, and social aspects of learning, has been theoretically well established."

"A view of SRL from a social cognitive learning perspective particularly emphasizes self-efficacy and strategy use as the two key factors in achieving self-regulation in academic learning [9]."

"Most studies on VLS focus on cognitive strategy use, while lack of concern is given on metacognitive (e.g., goal-setting) and affective factors (e.g., self-efficacy) in vocabulary learning [10]."

"It is necessary to investigate cognitive, metacognitive, and motivational aspects of vocabulary learning to provide a more comprehensive view of students' use of self-regulatory strategies in learning vocabulary."

3.1.3.2 Self-Regulated Learning Strategies

"Metacognition involves two aspects: knowledge of cognition (i.e., to know what, how, when, and why to use strategies) and regulation of cognition (i.e., metacognitive control strategies, such as goal-setting, self-monitoring, and self-evaluation) [11, 12]."

"Students must be motivated and able to self-initiate their efforts to use strategies during the learning process."

"The effective use of cognitive learning strategies occurs along with motivational aspects of learning, such as task interest and self-efficacy [13]."

"Though self-regulation involves all the learning strategies, the emphasis is on learners' self-initiation, i.e., learners' own strategic efforts to manage their own learning process [14]."

"The teaching of cognitive skills is insufficient to enable learners to manage to learn on their own; motivational factor (i.e., self-efficacy, task interest) should be addressed to support and sustain learners' use of self-regulatory strategies [15]."

3.1.3.3 Vocabulary Learning Strategies

"This definition not only involves both cognitive and metacognitive aspects of learning but also lays emphasis on using VLS to enhance vocabulary learning."

"Some researchers have tried to develop a taxonomy of vocabulary learning strategies."

"Metacognitive strategies involve selective attention and self-initiation in vocabulary learning; cognitive strategies refer to guessing, dictionary use, note-taking, rehearsal, encoding, and activation strategies, which are categorized into three stages of vocabulary learning process: initial handling, consolidation, and activation."

"Nation [16] identified learning strategies in terms of planning vocabulary learning; finding information about words; and establishing vocabulary knowledge."

3.1.3.4 Studies on Vocabulary Learning Strategies

"Gu and Johnson [17] who investigated the relationship between VLS and students' learning outcomes in English learning with 850 Chinese university learners of non-English majors revealed that students reported using a number of various VLS and holding negative beliefs to rote memorization strategies except for oral repetition."

"This was also confirmed by Fan [18] that more proficient learners acquired more knowledge by using a variety of strategies and planning their vocabulary learning."

"The mixed results of the above research on strategy use behaviour among Chinese EFL learners indicate that the various factors including personal (i.e., perceptions, language proficiency), educational background and culture affect students' strategy use."

"It has showed that the Chinese learners hold strong beliefs in memorization and consistently proved that metacognitive awareness, and strategy use are closely related to success in learning."

3.1.3.5 Context of the Study

"The study was conducted in Malaysia, where Chinese students from the Peoples' Republic of China (PRC) attempt to pursue their studies at the tertiary level in both public and private universities."

"International students who do not hold the necessary IELTS or TOEFL results are required to take the English Language Proficiency Program for International Students (ELPPIS) before proceeding with their studies at their respective faculties."

"The ELPPIS provides intensive English courses to prepare students for their academic study, with five levels ranging from elementary to higher intermediate."

3.1.3.6 Statement of the Problem

"English in Malaysia is used as a second language (ESL) rather than a Foreign language (EFL) in the Chinese context, providing Chinese international students more exposure to English language learning."

"The variety of academic tasks performed in English in a new learning context is certainly demanding for these Chinese English learners."

"It is necessary to investigate the Chinese EFL learners' use of strategies, as well as their current vocabulary knowledge and motivational beliefs in vocabulary learning, and to further provide useful information to direct instructional efforts to develop students' self-regulatory ability in learning."

"This study was conducted as a preliminary study to develop a strategy instructional program to enhance Chinese EFL learners' use of self-regulatory strategies."

3.1.3.7 Methodology

"For the purpose of the study, the existing instruments appropriate for the current research purposes have been adapted to assess learners' needs in terms of self-regulatory strategy use and motivational beliefs in vocabulary learning, as well as their current vocabulary knowledge level."

"A vocabulary level test developed by Nation (1990) was conducted to identify whether the students have acquired sufficient high- frequency words for their academic study."

"Focusing on passive vocabulary knowledge, the diagnostic test assessed whether learners have acquired sufficient high-frequency words for their study [16]."

"Before the questionnaire was delivered to the target group, a pilot test was conducted to 52 Chinese EFL learners studying the preuniversity English course in Malaysia to identify the level of reliability of the questions."

"The structured interview was conducted with the 14 students enrolled in semester II to obtain information on metacognitive strategy use and motivational beliefs on vocabulary learning."

3.1.3.8 Results and Discussion

"With reference to the four main questions, the following presents an analysis of the data to provide information about (1) learners' current level of passive vocabulary knowledge, (2) a profile of learners' needs in terms of cognitive and metacognitive control strategy use for vocabulary learning, and (3) the students' perceptions toward vocabulary learning."

"The participants did not report strategies, such as reviewing, grouping, and word parts while planning strategies in vocabulary learning, which might indicate the participants' lack of knowledge of various strategy uses."

"The results of the strategy survey also showed that students most frequently use the dictionary to help them with reading comprehension purposes, i.e., to look up the meaning of a word as the need arises rather than using the dictionary as a resource to exploit the information about a word to expand their vocabulary knowledge."

3.1.3.9 Summary and Implications

"This study as a preliminary study for developing strategy instruction for Chinese EFL learners has profiled self-regulatory strategy use, motivational beliefs, and vocabulary knowledge level of a group of Chinese learners studying at the University of Malaya."

"The findings of the study showed that there is a pressing need to enlarge the students' vocabulary knowledge to prepare them for university study; moreover, these learners lack knowledge and strategy use for learning vocabulary, especially metacognitive control strategy use."

"The findings of the study point to the need for learners to engage in more cognitive VLS and to enhance their metacognitive awareness and control of strategy use to improve their perception and motivation in vocabulary learning."

"The pedagogical implication of the study is that self-regulatory strategies including cognitive, metacognitive, affective aspects should be taught directly or indirectly to Chinese EFL learners to increase their strategy use awareness and effective use of strategies in vocabulary learning."

3.1.4 Effective Practices to Enhance Immigrant Kindergarteners' Second Language Vocabulary Learning Through Storybook Reading [76]

This is a machine-generated summary of:

Chlapana, Elissavet; Tafa, Eufimia: Effective practices to enhance immigrant kindergarteners' second language vocabulary learning through storybook reading [76]

Published in: Reading and Writing (2014)
Link to original: https://doi.org/10.1007/s11145-014-9510-7

If you want to cite the papers, please refer to the original.

For technical reasons we could not place the page where the original quote is coming from.

Abstract-Summary "This study examined the impact of direct instruction and interactive instruction on immigrant kindergarten children's vocabulary learning during storybook reading. (In the present study the terms "immigrants" and "second language learners" are used alternatively meaning kindergarteners from immigrant families who are in the process of acquiring a second language besides their mother tongue.) Eighty seven immigrant kindergarten children, aged 4–6 years old (mean = 61.68 months, standard deviations = .51) were recruited from 12 public kindergarten classrooms located in Crete."

"Target and non-target words were assessed by multiple choice vocabulary measure before and after the storybook readings."

"In the first experimental group, children were provided brief explanations of target words by direct instruction."

"In the second experimental group, children were involved actively in discussing target words according to interactive instruction techniques."

"In the control group stories were read without any explanation of target vocabulary."

"Results showed that interactive instruction was more beneficial on target vocabulary learning than direct instruction and the impact was greater for instructed words than for uninstructed ones."

"Children's initial level in Greek receptive vocabulary and target word knowledge had a significant impact on target word learning."

3.1.4.1 Introduction

"Research studies on second language vocabulary teaching have shown that teachers providing explicit explanations of the target word meanings during story readings contributes to young children's vocabulary learning [19–23]."

"Conclusions, the purpose of this study was to examine: (a) The impact of two different teaching practices, direct instruction and interactive instruction, on immigrant kindergarteners' second language vocabulary development. (b) The effectiveness of direct instruction and interactive instruction when implemented in whole group settings where monolingual and immigrant children from different nationalities are educated together. (c) If the effect of these two different teaching practices on vocabulary development is significantly differentiated by children's gender, age, cognitive development, and second language vocabulary level. (d) Whether the differences of compared practices on kindergartners' second language vocabulary learning are maintained in the long term."

3.1.4.2 Method

"During administration, children were asked to look at the 4 pictures on the page and point out the picture of the target word."

"Children in the control group experienced the 56 target words only through their exposure to the words as the first author read the storybooks."

"In experimental group 1, the first author taught the target words according to direct instruction without encouraging children's verbal participation in the teaching process."

"In experimental group 2, she taught the target words according to interactive instruction, using questions and prompts which encouraged children's active participation in the vocabulary teaching process."

"Pointing: children were asked questions that encouraged them to point at the word depiction in the book illustrations."

"Questions: children were asked open-type questions based on word meanings, book illustration and story plot, to encourage their cognitive involvement in the discussion of the story."

3.1.4.3 Results

"When all the non-significant main effects and interactions were removed, results showed that children's score improvement in the instructed word measure was significantly affected by: (a) the intervention program, $F(2, 74) = 29.65$, $p < .01$, (b) the children's initial Greek receptive vocabulary level, $F(1, 74) = 40.14$, $p < .01$, and (c) the children's pretest scores in the instructed words, $F(1, 74) = 29.65$, $p < .01$."

"Children in the direct and interactive instruction groups outperformed children in the control group with respect to the instructed words, and the differences in children's scores were significant."

"With respect to the significant interaction between the intervention program and gender, the ANCOVA Model showed that girls in the direct and interactive instruction groups outperformed boys in the instructed words and the differences between their scores were significant."

3.1.4.4 Discussion

"The purpose of the present study was to examine the impact of direct instruction and interactive instruction practices on immigrant kindergarteners' second language vocabulary development, and to show whether the effect of these practices was significantly differentiated by children's gender, age, cognitive skills, and second language vocabulary level."

"The results of the present study which showed the effect of immigrant children's initial Greek receptive vocabulary level on instructed word learning are also significant."

"With regard to the long-term effect of the compared practices, results showed that children in the interactive instruction group had significantly higher delayed posttest scores in the instructed words than children either in the direct instruction or in the control group."

"It seems than children's active involvement in the word explanation through interactive instruction techniques, which encourage them to relate the word definitions to book illustrations, story plot and background knowledge, constitutes a factor with significant short and long-term effects on vocabulary learning [24]."

3.1.5 Effects of Language Skills and Strategy Use on Vocabulary Learning Through Lexical Translation and Inferencing [77]

This is a machine-generated summary of:

Alahmadi, Alaa; Foltz, Anouschka: Effects of Language Skills and Strategy Use on Vocabulary Learning Through Lexical Translation and Inferencing [77]
Published in: Journal of Psycholinguistic Research (2020)
Link to original: https://doi.org/10.1007/s10936-020-09720-9

If you want to cite the papers, please refer to the original.
For technical reasons we could not place the page where the original quote is coming from.

Abstract-Summary "This study explores how vocabulary learning strategy usage and skills in the four language domains relate to participants' increase in vocabulary size and to the learning of specific vocabulary items over a certain period of time."

"Sixty-one advanced L1 Arabic L2 learners of English read target words in semi-authentic reading materials and were instructed to either guess the meaning from context or consult a dictionary."

"Pre- and delayed post-tests assessed vocabulary size and knowledge of the target vocabulary items."

3.1.5.1 Introduction

"We use a longitudinal design to investigate how learners' self-reported use of VLS and self-reported proficiency and language skills relate to their overall vocabulary size as well as the vocabulary learning that occurs over a certain period of time through lexical inferencing (guessing meaning from context) and lexical translation (looking words up in a dictionary)."

"Alahmadi [25], Alahmadi et al. [26] and Alsaif [27] found a statistically significant positive relationship between the strategy of guessing a word's meaning from the provided context and English vocabulary knowledge in terms of breadth in Saudi participants across a range of educational levels."

"Alqurashi [28] found that determination strategies, which include using monoligual or bililingual dictionaries and inferring meaning from context, showed the highest contribution (44%) to learners' vocabulary size, followed by social strategies (37%)."

3.1.5.2 Current Study

"We investigate how VLS usage and language skills in the four domains relate to participants' increase in vocabulary size and to how many words participants learned through guessing and dictionary use over the course of the study."

"The current study aims to answer the following research questions (RQs): RQ1: Is participants' VLS usage related to their vocabulary size in general and to the increase in their vocabulary knowledge over the course of the study?"

"RQ2: Is participants' VLS usage related to how well they learn the words through guessing or dictionary use throughout the duration of the study?"

"RQ3: Are participants' self-assessed English language skills related to their vocabulary size in general and to the increase in their vocabulary knowledge over the course of the study?"

"RQ4: Are participants' self-assessed English language skills related to how well they learn the words through guessing or dictionary use throughout the duration of the study?"

3.1.5.3 Methodology

"Participants translated 24 target and 24 control words."

"Difficulty levels were sufficiently high to allow for learning, with participants in the norming study correctly translating only a minority of both target and control words."

"After giving informed consent, which included access to students' academic Grade Point Average (GPA), participants completed the English language self-assessment questionnaire, the word translation task, and finally the XK_Lex vocabulary breadth size test (cf. Alahmadi and Foltz, under revision, for more detailed information)."

"Prior to training, participants were distributed into a low and high proficiency group based on their GPA, their vocabulary size, and the word translation task."

"Participants again completed the word translation task and the XK_Lex vocabulary size test."

"Participants first completed the word translation task, then the XK_Lex vocabulary size test, and finally the VLS questionnaire."

3.1.5.4 Results

"The final model revealed a significant main effect of bilingual dictionary use on overall vocabulary gain (estimate = 333.4; SE = 114.6; t = 2.91; p = 0.005), indicating that learners who reported using a bilingual dictionary more often increased their vocabulary knowledge more over the course of the study than learners who reported using a bilingual dictionary less often."

"The final model for the inferencing condition revealed a significant main effect of guessing from context on learning words through inferencing during training (estimate = 0.197; SE = 0.086; t = 2.28; p = 0.026), such that participants who reported using the lexical inferencing from context strategy more often learned more words when asked to engage in inferencing during the study than participants who reported using this strategy less regularly."

3.1.5.5 Discussion

"The second finding is consistent with various previous studies, such as Alahmadi et al. [26], Alsaif [27] and Al Qahtani [29], who found a significant positive relationship between participants' inferencing strategy use and their vocabulary size for learners of various proficiency levels."

"The third finding is consistent with studies that find a positive relationship between bilingual dictionary use or determination strategies more generally and vocabulary size [30, 31]."

"The current study goes beyond these previous results in showing that frequent self-reported use of a bilingual dictionary contributed to learners' vocabulary size increase over a certain period of time."

"We found no evidence for Hamzah et al. [31] claim that the relationship between bilingual dictionary use and vocabulary size in previous studies is due to learners' inadequate knowledge of other VLS."

"Our third result finds that learners who engaged in note taking more regularly increased their vocabulary size less over the course of the study than participants who reported using this strategy less frequently."

3.1.5.6 Conclusion

"The current results highlight that vocabulary acquisition through inferencing, but not through dictionary look-up, depends on learners' familiarity with this strategy."

"Interventions that familiarize learners with inferencing strategies may therefore positively impact word learning in a foreign language."

"We suggest that familiarity with inferencing strategies can benefit learners and that the relationship between note taking and vocabulary acquisition warrants further investigation."

3.1.6 The Effectiveness of L2 Vocabulary Instruction: A Meta-Analysis [78]

This is a machine-generated summary of:

Yousefi, Mohammad Hossein; Biria, Reza: The effectiveness of L2 vocabulary instruction: a meta-analysis [78]
Published in: Asian-Pacific Journal of Second and Foreign Language Education (2018)
Link to original: https://doi.org/10.1186/s40862-018-0062-2

If you want to cite the papers, please refer to the original.
For technical reasons we could not place the page where the original quote is coming from.

Abstract-Summary "The purpose of the present meta-analysis is to the investigate the overall effectiveness of L2 vocabulary instruction and to find the moderator variables affecting its effectiveness."

"After conducting Q test of heterogeneity, a number of moderator variables were examined; context of instruction, publication type, age and L2 learners' proficiency level."

"That (a) studies conducted in foreign language contexts generated larger effect sizes than ones conducted in SL contexts. (b)intermediated learners show a larger effect size than advanced and elementary students. (c) child learners were better than adult learners in Learning L2 vocabulary. (d) Published studies generated larger effect size than doctoral dissertations. (e) employing "posters" for teaching L2 vocabulary items generated higher effect size than reading activities, CALL, and songs. (f) abstract words generated higher effect size than concrete ones."

3.1.6.1 Introduction

"A number of studies have provided evidence that glosses are effective in helping learners learn new lexical items in a second language [32, 33], for example, the results of [34] indicated that glossing had a positive effect on L2 vocabulary learning."

"Computer-assisted language learning in L2 vocabulary was shown to have positive effects with a medium effect size (d = 0.745, p = 0.000).The results of Abraham's meta-analysis [35] showed that computer-mediated glosses had an overall medium effect on second language reading comprehension and a large effect on incidental vocabulary learning."

"Although the meta-analyses on L2 vocabulary teaching have highly contributed to the field of instructed L2 vocabulary learning, the effectiveness of receptive L2 vocabulary learning remains a relatively under-researched line of inquiry in the literature."

"The study attempts to evaluate the moderator variables such as context of instruction, publication type, the age of the participants, and the L2 learners' proficiency level on the L2 vocabulary learning, type of technology, word type."

3.1.6.2 Methodology

"The criteria stipulated for the inclusion of the studies for the current meta-analysis were as follows; 1) Dependent variable, in this meta-analysis, is second or foreign language vocabulary acquisition."

"2) Studies included for the current meta-analysis should be experimental or quasi-experimental."

"5) The current meta-analysis included both published and unpublished studies."

"Among unpublished studies, doctoral dissertations will be included in the current meta-analysis to the exclusions of the proceedings of the conferences."

"Studies published before 2004 were excluded from the present meta-analysis."

"Coding measurement procedures and research settings would enable the reviewer to assess whether effect size estimates had been affected by the choice of instrument or the location of the study [36]."

"For the present meta-analysis, the coding scheme was constructed by reviewing previously published meta-analyses and based on the research questions that guided the present study."

3.1.6.3 Results

"The second research question asked, "To what extent the effect sizes varied across studies?"".

"It indicated that the null hypothesis should be rejected, Q (16) = 59.94, $p < .01$, finding that effect sizes varied significantly across studies."

"The answer to the second research question is that there is sizable variation of effect sizes across studies."

"This type of distribution would reflect the tendency for smaller studies with larger than average effect sizes, making them more likely to achieve statistical significance, to be published [37]."

"When publication bias is not present, the studies should be distributed symmetrically around the average effect size because of random sampling error."

"Studies with larger sample sizes appear towards the upper portion of the funnel and are relatively evenly distributed about the mean, with the graph indicating that medium and larger scale studies with medium effect sizes were well represented."

3.1.6.4 Moderator Variable Analysis

"A small to medium effect (d = 0.53) for Second language contexts and large effect for foreign language settings (d = 0.96) were obtained."

"The difference between foreign language and second language contexts was not statistically significant (Q = 3.02, df = 1, P = 0.08)."

"Ten primary studies were conducted targeting intermediate l2 learners and 5 studies included participants in elementary level of L2 proficiency."

"With respect to L2 proficiency level, small effect size (d = 0.53) was obtained for both advanced and elementary levels (d = 0.54)."

"Large effect size (d = 0.95) was gained for intermediate L2 learners."

"CALL technology produced the effect size of (d = 0.68, k = 7)."

"The smallest effect size was gained for studies that employed song to teach the target words (d = 0.47, k = 0.47)."

3.1.6.5 General Discussion

"The mean effect size associated with the studies conducted in FL contexts was larger than those conducted in SL contexts, indicating that L2 vocabulary instruction was more effective in FL contexts than in SL ones (d = 0.96 vs. d = 0.53)."

"The results of Huang's [38] meta-analysis showed that the vocabulary learning of language learners with low proficiency levels and vocabulary sizes may benefit more from L1 textual glosses than those who have higher proficiency levels and larger vocabulary sizes."

"Future research should examine other potential moderators, including setting (e.g., instructed vs. naturalistic setting), instructional variables (e.g., instructional tasks and activities), teacher orientation (e.g., beliefs and attitudes), and L2 learner variables (e.g., type of motivation, cognitive style, and learning strategies) that may influence the effectiveness of L2 vocabulary instruction."

3.1.6.6 Conclusion

"The research synthesis indicates that l2 vocabulary instruction was effective and given the significance of vocabulary, L2 vocabulary teaching should be incorporated as indispensable part of L2 syllabus."

"What remains unresolved, here, is the question of what factors and variables enhance L2 vocabulary development more effectively than the other variables."

"To gain such an insight, we call for constructing L2 vocabulary models and hypotheses that provide syllabus designers and language teachers with cost-effective techniques of teaching L2 vocabulary items."

3.1.7 Music as a Mnemonic Device for Foreign Vocabulary Learning [79]

This is a machine-generated summary of:

Chen, I-Shan Jenny: Music as a Mnemonic Device for Foreign Vocabulary Learning [79]
Published in: English Teaching & Learning (2020)
Link to original: https://doi.org/10.1007/s42321-020-00049-z

If you want to cite the papers, please refer to the original.
For technical reasons we could not place the page where the original quote is coming from.

Abstract-Summary "It is of value to determine whether it is beneficial to incorporate music when young EFL (English as a foreign language) learners acquire new vocabulary."

"The research attempted to determine whether music can help young EFL learners with vocabulary acquisition and if so, which pedagogical practice leads to the optimal gains."

"Results found in this study proved that the better acquisition of novel vocabulary in EFL learning could be achieved with the help of familiar melodies, with "chanting" and "music video with caption" methods being the most effective and lead to immediate and prolonged learning."

3.1.7.1 Introduction

"Of neuroimaging studies (e.g., [39–42]), researchers have provided empirical evidence that areas of the brains underlying the processing of music and language are interconnected; incongruities in a piece of music are found to be processed in the Broca area—the same area responsible for language processing."

"In recent years, researchers and practitioners have empirically established that music can effectively serve as a platform for various aspects of language learning, including enhancing students' motivation and attention (e.g., [43]) and learning novel words (e.g., [44, 45])."

"Researches have indicated that language learners seem to retain textual information longer when accompanied with melody than just learning the text without music [45–49]."

"Existing research on music and language learning is predominantly based on first language (L1) and second language (L2) learners, who continue to have access to native input beyond the study settings (e.g., [39, 45, 49–51])."

3.1.7.2 Literature Review

"To substantiate the above view, Wallace [49] conducted another experiment in which the learners were assigned to two music conditions: (1) familiar tune condition, where the learners learned a novel ballad sung to the same melody condition three times; and (2) unfamiliar tune condition, where the learners learned the same ballad sung with three different melodies."

"The finding, thus, provided affirmative evidence for the facilitative role of familiar tunes in retaining the novel's lexical and textual information; music only became effective retrieval cues for the target linguistic materials when the melody or tune is sufficiently learned and/or is familiar to the learners."

"It remains unclear if familiar music tunes/songs can be used to facilitate language learning and retention of words of different nature: novel vs. partially learned (unfamiliar) words."

"Of the immediate test, the researchers posited that music with a familiar tune or melody was an effective mnemonic device for short-term retention of novel words."

3.1.7.3 Methodology

"Under the "chanting" condition, with the help of a tambourine, the teacher guided the participants to chant the lyrics of the song with no melody (similar to the practice of Jazz Chants); the music treatment was mainly administered to students through singular (audio-only) modality."

"The participants under the no intervention condition were taught the vocabulary at the beginning and simply tested at the end with no music intervention."

"Despite the aforementioned differences in how the input was provided, the participants in the four interventional groups (conditions 1–4) received comparable length of music treatment every week (20 min every week)."

"Only the 18 target words were the focus of the study; a point was awarded to each participant for correct answer of each target word, yielding the highest possible score of 18 points for the multiple-choice test."

3.1.7.4 Results

"After undergoing the treatment conditions under investigation, the participants' mean scores on the immediate vocabulary test in groups of chanting, singing, music-video-only, music-video-plus-caption, and control are 7.14, 7.65, 6.39, 7.2, and 6.5, respectively."

"With regard to the delayed vocabulary test, the descriptive statistics showed that the participants assigned to the "chanting group" received the highest mean raw score (mean = 8.18); the participants assigned to the "music-video-plus-caption" group also had comparable (satisfying) performance, as indicated by their mean raw score on the delayed vocabulary test (mean = 7.55)—a result reminiscent of the scenario observed in the immediate vocabulary test."

"In light of this, Tukey's HSD test was performed and showed that there was a significant difference in the participants' performance between the "chanting" and the control groups ($t = 4.29$, $p < .005$), and between the "music-video plus-caption" and the control groups ($t = 3.16$, $p < .05$)."

3.1.7.5 Discussion

"Examinations of the participants' data from the immediate and delayed tests revealed that rhythm (as provided by the "chanting" condition) and melody (as provided by the "singing" and "music-video-plus-caption" conditions) did not seem to provide the same memory scaffold for the target vocabulary, with the former (rhythm as provided under the chanting condition) playing a more effective role in retaining the observed vocabulary gain."

"Another alternative desirable (i.e., second best) music-based treatment is the "music-video-plus-caption" condition; its positive impact is captured in all immediate and delayed vocabulary measures, thus establishing the facilitative role of multimodal input as provided by the use of multimedia."

"Although the most desirable music-based treatment conditions for immediate and delayed vocabulary gains are not exactly the same ("singing" and "chanting" for immediate and delayed gains, respectively), this study argues that chanting may be a better option based on Peretz et al. [52] account noted above."

3.1.7.6 Conclusion

"While it is common practice to use music in children's EFL classrooms, there are many different forms."

"In this day and age, new devices and technologies are being utilized in classrooms; however, are they necessary and do they necessarily result in better learning?"

"Even chanting, with the absence of a melody, an even more basic practice, produced surprisingly exceptional results in the receptive form-meaning vocabulary knowledge."

3.1.8 An English Vocabulary Learning Support System for the Learner's Sustainable Motivation [80]

This is a machine-generated summary of:

Hasegawa, Tatsuhito; Koshino, Makoto; Ban, Hiromi: An English vocabulary learning support system for the learner's sustainable motivation [80]
Published in: SpringerPlus (2015)
Link to original: https://doi.org/10.1186/s40064-015-0792-2

If you want to cite the papers, please refer to the original.
For technical reasons we could not place the page where the original quote is coming from.

Abstract-Summary "In English vocabulary learning, continuation is an important factor; however, many learners are not good at continuing learning because they tend to prefer amusement or rest."

"We especially focused on English vocabulary learning, and described an approach for learners who have difficulty with continuing learning."

3.1.8.1 Introduction

"Considering an e-learning environment where mobile devices are used, the term "mobile learning," or m-learning, is also focused on [53]."

"We considered that using a smartphone is effective for independent learning such as English vocabulary memorization because a learner can use the smartphone anytime and anywhere when the learner has only a little time."

"In English vocabulary learning, continuation is an important factor, although, many learners are not good at continuing learning."

"Focusing on [2] learners, we developed an English vocabulary learning application for the learner's sustainable motivation by gamification and cloud intelligent techniques utilizing characteristics of smartphones."

3.1.8.2 Related Works

"E-learning has an advantage that a learner can learn alone anytime and anywhere; however, it also has a disadvantage that it is difficult for the learner to maintain his/her motivation."

"We clarify a position and a characteristic of our study, through considerations of related works which enhance the learners' motivation in the e-learning environment."

"In order to maintain the learners' motivation, we focused on gamification techniques."

"We considered that utilizing gamification techniques in e-learning has a positive influence on the user's learning motivation."

"We considered that difficulty settings of questions are also important to maintain the learner's motivation."

"Focusing on the independent learning of English vocabulary memorization, we developed an m-learning application utilizing gamification techniques for keeping the learner's motivation."

3.1.8.3 Proposal System Design

"Task is a question or problem in the game to help learners to absorb the learning content (i.e., English word questions in this case), and it should be designed with different levels."

"This idea may be effective for learners who have little motivation to learn; however, the game with a few learning features has disadvantages for our concept as follows: (1) it increases wasteful time for learning; (2) learners will get tired of learning if the learners get tired of the video game; (3) the pain of learning in itself is not decreased; therefore, in our application, we selected simple English vocabulary learning in a repetition style with some gamification factors."

"This application shows a learner's efforts such as the number of answered questions, the number of correct answers, and the difficulty of learned questions."

3.1.8.4 Question Selection by Estimating Learner's Skills

"We propose a new method that estimates whether the learner has already mastered a word; accordingly, setting a suitable percentage of mastered words and unmastered words improves the learner's motivation."

"Rounding V a l u e(u,w) to the nearest whole number, when the rounded value is 1, it means that the learner u has already mastered the word w. S i m i l a r i t y(u,v) means the degree of similarity between the learner u and v. These are calculated as follows, where u is a learner about whom we estimate whether a word w has already been mastered, V' is a group of 10 learners' who have the highest degree of similarity of all learners, r_{vw} is the latest answer for the word w by the learner v (True is 1 and False is 0), and $|W'|$ is the number of words which the learner u has already learned."

3.1.8.5 Our Application Evaluation

"We considered that the learners felt that time trial challenge was more characteristic than weak point learning because the number of answers of "Neither agree nor disagree" in the time trial challenge was significantly fewer than that in the weak point learning."

"About content no.11, the ratio of "Agree" was 73.1% which was the highest ratio of all; therefore, most learners are especially interested in the clear points and ranking function."

"About content no.13 and no.14, both these contents have a lower ratio of "Agree"; further, the ratio of "Disagree" in no.14 was 61.5% which was the highest ratio of all; therefore, most learners were not interested in submitting their score to SNS services, and they thought that the SNS function did not affect their motivation in this case."

3.1.8.6 Conclusion

"Focusing on motivated learners who cannot continue learning, we developed an English vocabulary learning support system for sustainable motivation."

"This application is equipped with the necessary functions for English vocabulary learning."

"We believe that we have succeeded in making an application that supports the growth of self-sufficient learners in the following steps: (1) learner who cannot continue learning; (2) learner who enjoys our application in terms of gamification; (3) learner who is interested in self-growth; (4) self-sufficient learner."

"As future efforts, we will evaluate the degree of continuation using our application."

3.1.9 *The Effects of Vocabulary Enhancement Exercises and Group Dynamic Assessment on Word Learning Through Lexical Inferencing [81]*

This is a machine-generated summary of:

Bahramlou, Khosro; Esmaeili, Adel: The Effects of Vocabulary Enhancement Exercises and Group Dynamic Assessment on Word Learning Through Lexical Inferencing [81]
Published in: Journal of Psycholinguistic Research (2019)
Link to original: https://doi.org/10.1007/s10936-019-09638-x

If you want to cite the papers, please refer to the original.
For technical reasons we could not place the page where the original quote is coming from.

Abstract-Summary "The study aimed to explore the effect of group dynamic assessment on word learning through lexical inferencing and to compare it to that of vocabulary enhancement exercises."

"Of each treatment session, the first group engaged in lexical inferencing of the underlined words within group dynamic assessment framework."

"The second group did two vocabulary exercises for each target word."

"The third group engaged in lexical inferencing of target words through group dynamic assessment framework and also did one vocabulary exercise for each target word."

"The results showed that in terms of gains in depth and size of vocabulary knowledge the first and the second groups were not significantly different."

"It was concluded that group dynamic assessment is as effective as vocabulary exercises in enhancing word learning through lexical inferencing and that the combination of group dynamic assessment and vocabulary exercises could enhance word learning through lexical inferencing even more."

3.1.9.1 Introduction

"In Wesche and Paribakht's [54] view, lexical inferencing is primarily a reading comprehension strategy through which some words might be learnt as a byproduct."

"In naturalistic lexical inferencing studies, the learners are not informed of the presence of unfamiliar words within the texts."

"To improve word learning through lexical inferencing, interventionist lexical inferencing studies were developed."

"Another hypothesis was forwarded to improve word learning through lexical inferencing."

"The current study aimed to explore the effects of VE exercises and GDA on the amount of word learning through lexical inferencing."

"Among VE exercises, GDA, and GDA plus VE exercises, which condition would lead to more word learning through lexical inferencing?"

3.1.9.2 Theoretical Background

"The instructor could intervene in the inferencing process and offer mediational hints to the learners who cannot independently infer the meanings of unfamiliar words."

"A two-way interactive relationship would be developed between the teacher and the learner in which the learner could also initiate questions, seek feedback on his/her inferences, and ask for more explicit mediational hints if needed."

"GDA aims to co-construct the ZPD of a group of learners in learning tasks which are beyond the independent control of all individual members of the group."

"The teacher may interact with individual learners; however, he/she would quickly shift from these primary interactants to secondary interactants to keep the task aligned with the ZPD of the whole group."

"In cumulative GDA, the teacher engages in a sequence of one-to-one interactions with individual members of the group to help the whole group to gain mastery over the task objective."

3.1.9.3 Review of Literature

"A number of interventionist lexical inferencing studies have shown that directing learners' attention toward the unfamiliar words through annotations, marginal glosses, production tasks, use of bilingual dictionaries, or VE activities could substantially enhance word learning through lexical inferencing [55–64]."

"Regarding the effect of DA on word learning through lexical inferencing, Hayes [65] conducted a lexical inferencing study with 28 fourth grade L1 learners."

"She began with the first unfamiliar word of the text and asked the learner to provide its meaning."

"When the provided meaning was incorrect, the researcher provided the first mediational prompt by pointing to the word in the text and asked the learner to give the word meaning."

"In their experiment group which received CDA treatment, when the selected option was incorrect, the program drew on the text and presented four successive mediational hints arranged from the most implicit to the most explicit until the learner inferred the word meaning correctly or the meaning was provided by the program."

3.1.9.4 Method

"This range of vocabulary knowledge was selected so that some of the texts' words would be unfamiliar to the learners."

"At least 95% of the text's words should be familiar to the learner."

"The words for which contextual clues could be located in the text or in the knowledge of the intended learners were selected as lexical inferencing targets."

"Of each session, in the GDA group the teacher required one learner to read aloud the paragraph which contained the first target word."

"Of each session, in the VE group each learner received a sheet of paper which contained two exercises for each of the text's target words."

"After a 5-min break, each member of the 'GDA + VE' group received a sheet of paper which contained one exercise for each of the text's target words."

3.1.9.5 Results

"Test of between-subjects effects showed that on the dependent variables, group means were significantly different: $F_{Learning}(2, 42) = 4.70$, $p < 0.014$; partial $\eta^2 = 0.18$; $F_{Retention}(2, 42) = 7.22$, $p < 0.002$; partial $\eta^2 = 0.25$."

"The mean scores of GDA and VE groups on learning and retention variables did not differ significantly: GDA-VE mean difference on learning variable = 0.67, $p < 0.797$; GDA-VE mean difference on retention variable = 1.40, $p < 0.392$."

"The mean scores of 'GDA + VE' group were significantly higher than those of the GDA and VE groups: GDAVE-GDA mean difference on learning variable = 6.00, $p < 0.025$; GDAVE-VE mean difference on learning variable = 6.67, $p < 0.013$; GDAVE-GDA mean difference on retention variable = 7.80, $p < 0.000$; GDAVE-VE mean difference on retention variable = 6.40, $p < 0.000$."

3.1.9.6 Discussion and Conclusion

"This study investigated the effect of GDA on word learning through lexical inferencing and compared it to that of VE exercises."

"In the GDA and VE groups, mean gains in size of vocabulary knowledge (learning posttest) amounted to 53.32% and 51.54% of the target words, respectively."

"To naturalistic lexical inferencing studies which reported less than 20% gains in knowledge of target words in immediate posttests [66–72], VE exercises and GDA lead to substantially more vocabulary learning."

"Since vocabulary gains in GDA and VE groups of this study were not significantly different, it could be concluded that, just like VE exercises, GDA could enhance word learning through lexical inferencing."

"This measure helped promote the learners' developing lexical inferencing ability and enhance word learning through this strategy."

"DA procedures helped promote developing inferencing abilities and VE exercises enhanced the salience and cognitive processing of the target words."

3.1.10 Vocabulary Learning from Reading: Examining Interactions Between Task and Learner Related Variables [82]

This is a machine-generated summary of:

Wu, Xiaoli; Lowyck, Joost; Sercu, Lies; Elen, Jan: Vocabulary learning from reading: examining interactions between task and learner related variables [82]
Published in: European Journal of Psychology of Education (2012)
Link to original: https://doi.org/10.1007/s10212-012-0113-x

If you want to cite the papers, please refer to the original.
For technical reasons we could not place the page where the original quote is coming from.

Abstract-Summary "In the field of second and foreign language learning, how various task characteristics affect language learning has been the focus of many recent studies."

"Much of this research examined the relationship between task characteristics and task performance without fully taking into account learner related variables."

"The present study aimed to assess task complexity and sequence in relation to the learner related variables drawn from the social cognitive perspective of self-regulated learning, i.e. self-efficacy beliefs and frequency of learning strategy use, as they were applied to two versions of vocabulary learning from reading tasks."

"Results reveal a significant effect of task sequence on vocabulary learning self-efficacy beliefs, frequency of learning strategy use and task performance, and a significant interaction effect of sequence with task complexity."

3.1.10.1 Introduction

"The theoretical and empirical literature on information processing (such as the cognitive complexity dimension of the task), as well as the literature on social cognitive constructs from mainstream educational psychology (such as self-efficacy beliefs), have not produced substantial progress in the domain of L2 vocabulary learning."

"It is reasonable to expect that tasks at varying levels of complexity may affect learners' self-efficacy beliefs and demand different cognitive learning strategies."

"What effect does the designed task at different levels of complexity have on learners' self-efficacy beliefs, learning strategy use and task performance?"

"We were also interested to know if there was a main effect of task sequence and/or an interaction effect of task complexity and task sequence on learners' self-efficacy beliefs, use of learning strategies and task performance."

3.1.10.2 Method

"The vocabulary learning from reading task required participants to read a text passage, understand the content of the text, learn the target words from the provided text and answer true or false comprehension questions."

"A vocabulary learning self-efficacy scale was also developed to elicit participants' judgements of their confidence that they possess the skills appropriate for performing vocabulary learning tasks from reading."

"Participants were asked to rate their self-efficacy for these aspects of vocabulary learning for each task version."

"Participants were asked to complete both the task self-efficacy and vocabulary learning self-efficacy scales on this task."

"In order to examine if there was a main effect on self-efficacy beliefs, learning strategies and vocabulary post-tests for text, task complexity and the possible interaction effect for the between-subject variables task sequence and task complexity, MANOVA was used as the main statistical procedure in the data analysis."

3.1.10.3 Results

"The text variable did not have any effect on task self-efficacy, vocabulary learning self-efficacy, learning strategy use and post-test score."

"With regard to the effect of task complexity on self-efficacy beliefs, learning strategy use and task performance, univariate tests showed only a significant effect on learning strategy use [$F(1, 275) = 31.83$, $p < 0.001$, partial eta squared is 0.10]."

"The main analyses reveal a substantial effect of task complexity on learning strategy use; however, we did not find a significant effect of task complexity on self-efficacy beliefs and performance measures."

"With regard to the effect of sequence on the dependent variables, the results showed significant effects on vocabulary learning self-efficacy $F(1, 275) = 3.80$, $p < 0.05$, learning strategy use $F(1, 275) = 4.43$, $p < 0.05$, and task performance $F(1, 275) = 21.79$, $p < 0.001$."

3.1.10.4 Discussion and Conclusion

"The current study examined the effect of task complexity and the possible interaction effect of task complexity and task sequence on students' self-efficacy beliefs, learning strategy use and task performance with two versions of vocabulary learning from reading tasks that were manipulated along the complexity dimension +/– single task demand."

"Regarding the first main research question on the effect of task complexity on the learner related variables, contrary to our hypotheses, no significant effect from task complexity was found for students' task self-efficacy beliefs, vocabulary learning self-efficacy beliefs and task performance; a significant negative effect of task complexity was only found for learning strategy use."

"Results from the current study showed a significant main effect of task sequence and a significant interaction effect of task complexity and task sequence on students' vocabulary learning self-efficacy beliefs, frequency of learning strategy use and task performance."

Bibliography

1. Herlocker, J. L., Konstan, J. A., Borchers, A., & Riedl, J. (1999). An algorithmic framework for performing collaborative filtering. In *Proceedings of the 22nd annual international ACM SIGIR conference on research and development in information retrieval* (pp. 230–237). doi: https://doi.org/10.1145/312624.312682 .
2. Resnick, P., Iacovou, N., Suchak, M., Bergstrom, P., & Riedl, J. (1994). GroupLens: An open architecture for collaborative filtering of netnews. In *Proceedings of the 1994 ACM conference on computer supported cooperative work* (pp. 175–186). doi: https://doi.org/10.1145/192844.192905 .
3. Anderson, A., & Lynch, T. (1988). *Listening*. Oxford University Press.
4. Jafari, S. (2019). The effect of scaffolding on the vocabulary improvement of EFL Iranian language learner. *International Journal of English Literature and Social Sciences (IJELS), 4*(2), 206–210.
5. Khajeh Khosravi, S. (2017). The effect of symmetrical scaffolding on the reading comprehension of Iranian EFL learners. *International Journal of Psychological and Brain Sciences, 2*(4), 95–99.
6. Talebinejad, M. R., & Akhgar, F. (2015). The impact of teacher scaffolding on Iranian intermediate EFL learner's listening comprehension achievement. *Theory and Practice in Language Studies, 5*(5), 110–125.
7. Izanlu, M., & Feyli, M. (2015). The effects of symmetrical and asymmetrical scaffolding on university students' grammar acquisition. *Journal of Advances in English Language Teaching, 3*(6), 106–115.
8. Yongqi, G. P. (2003). Vocabulary learning in a second language: Person, task, context and strategies. *TESL-EJ, 7*(2), 1–26.
9. Zimmerman, B. J. (1989). A social cognitive view of self- regulated academic learning. *Journal of Educational Psychology, 81*(3), 329–339.
10. Rasekh, Z. E., & Ranjbary, R. (2003). Metacognitive strategy training for vocabulary learning. *Journal of TESL- EJ, 7*(2).
11. Weinstein, C. E., & Mayer, R. E. (1986). The teaching of learning strategies. In M. C. Wittrock (Ed.), *Handbook of research on teaching* (3rd ed., pp. 315–327). Macmillan.
12. Pintrich, P. R. (2002). The role of metacognitive knowledge in learning, teaching, and assessing. *Theory Into Practice, 41*(4), 219–225.
13. Weinstein, C. E., Husman, J., & Dierking, D. R. (2005). Self- regulation interventions with a focus on learning strategies. In M. Bockaerts, P. R. Pintrich, & M. Zeidner (Eds.), *Handbook of self-regulation* (pp. 727–747). Academic.
14. Zimmerman, B. J., & Risemberg, R. (1997). Self-regulatory dimensions of academic learning and motivation. In G. D. Phye (Ed.), *Handbook of academic learning: Construction of knowledge* (pp. 105–125). Academic.

15. Schunk, D. H., & Ertmer, P. A. (2005). Self-regulation and academic learning: Self-efficacy enhancing interventions. In M. Boekaerts, P. R. Pintrich, & M. Zeidner (Eds.), *Handbook of self-regulation* (pp. 631–649). Academic.
16. Nation, I. S. P. (2001). *Learning vocabulary in another language*. Cambridge University Press.
17. Gu, Y., & Johnson, R. K. (1996). Vocabulary learning strategies and language learning outcomes. *Language Learning, 46*, 643–679.
18. Fan, M. Y. (2003). Frequency of use, perceived usefulness, and actual usefulness of second language vocabulary strategies: A study of Hong Kong learners. *The Modern Language Journal, 87*(2), 222–241.
19. Biemiller, A., & Boote, C. (2006). An effective method for building vocabulary in primary grades. *Journal of Educational Psychology, 98*, 44–62.
20. Collins, M. F. (2010). ELL preschoolers' English vocabulary acquisition from storybook reading. *Early Childhood Research Quarterly, 25*, 84–97.
21. Justice, L. M., Meier, J., & Walpole, S. (2005). Learning new words from storybooks: An efficacy study with at-risk kindergartners. *Language, Speech, and Hearing Services in Schools, 36*(1), 17–32. https://doi.org/10.1044/0161-1461(2005/003)
22. Lugo-Neris, M., Wood Jackson, C., & Goldstein, H. (2010). Facilitating vocabulary acquisition of young English language learners. *Language, Speech, and Hearing Services in Schools, 41*, 314–327.
23. Penno, J. F., Wilkinson, I. A., & Moore, D. W. (2002). Vocabulary acquisition from teacher explanation and repeated listening to stories: Do they overcome the Matthew effect? *Journal of Educational Psychology, 94*(1), 23–33.
24. Anthony, A. R. B. (2008). Output strategies for English-language learners: Theory to practice. *The Reading Teacher, 61*, 472–482.
25. Alahmadi, A. (2015). *Exploring vocabulary learning strategies of Saudi undergraduate EFL students at King Abdulaziz University and its relationship to their vocabulary size* (Unpublished PhD thesis). Bangor University.
26. Alahmadi, A., Shank, C., & Foltz, A. (2018). Vocabulary learning strategies and vocabulary size: Insights from educational level and learner styles. *Vocabulary Learning and Instruction, 7*(1), 1–21. https://doi.org/10.7820/vli.v07.1.alahmadi
27. AlSaif, A. (2011). *Investigating vocabulary input and explaining vocabulary uptake among EFL learners in Saudi Arabia* (Unpublished PhD thesis). Swansea University.
28. Alqurashi, N. (2013). *Vocabulary learning strategies of Saudi undergraduate EFL students at Taif University and its relation to their vocabulary size* (Unpublished MA thesis). Anglia Ruskin University.
29. Al Qahtani, M. (2005). *The use of vocabulary learning strategies by EFL learners at three different educational levels* (Unpublished PhD thesis). University of Essex.
30. Hamzah, M. S. G., Kafipour, R., & Abdullah, S. K. (2009). Vocabulary learning strategies of Iranian undergraduate EFL students and its relation to their vocabulary size. *European Journal of Social Sciences, 11*(1), 39–50.
31. Komol, T., & Sripetpun, W. (2011). Vocabulary learning strategies employed by undergraduate students and its relationship to their vocabulary knowledge. In *The 3rd international conference on humanities and social sciences*. Faculty of Liberal Arts, Prince of Songkla University (pp. 1–18). Faculty of Liberal Arts, Prince of Songkla University.
32. Bowles, M. A. (2004). L2 glossing: To CALL or not to CALL. *Hispania, 87*, 541–552.
33. Cheng, Y., & Good, R. L. (2009). L1 glosses: Effects on EFL learners' reading comprehension and vocabulary retention. *Reading in a Foreign Language, 21*, 119–142.
34. Ko, H. M. (2012). Glossing and second language vocabulary learning. *TESOL Quarterly., 46*(1), 56–79.
35. Abraham, L. B. (2008). Computer-mediated glosses in second language reading comprehension and vocabulary learning: A meta-analysis. *Computer Assisted Language Learning, 21*(3), 199–226.

36. Ellis, P. (2010). *The essential guide to effect sizes. Statistical power, meta- analysis and the interpretation of research result*. Cambridge University Press.
37. Borenstein, M., Hedges, L. V., Higgins, J. P. T., & Rothstein, H. (2009). *Computing effect sizes for meta-analysis*. Wiley.
38. Huang, S. F. (2010). *Effects of tasks and glosses on L2 incidental vocabulary learning: Meta-analysis, unpublished doctoral dissertation*. Texas A&M University.
39. Boll-Avetisyan, N., Bhatara, A., Unger, A., Nazzi, T., & Höhle, B. (2016). Effects of experience with L2 and music on rhythmic grouping by French listeners. *Bilingualism: Language and Cognition, 19*(5), 971–986.
40. Levitin, D. J., & Menon, V. (2003). Musical structure is processed in "language" areas of the brain: A possible role for Brodmann area 47 in temporal coherence. *NeuroImage, 20*(4), 2142–2152.
41. Maess, B., Koelsch, S., Gunter, T. C., & Friederici, A. D. (2001). Musical syntax is processed in Broca's area: An MEG study. *Nature Neuroscience, 4*, 540–545.
42. Turker, S., Reiterer, S. M., Schneider, P., & Seither-Preisler, A. (2018). Th neuroanatomical correlates of foreign language aptitude. In S. M. Reiterer (Ed.), *Exploring language aptitude: Views from psychology, the language sciences, and cognitive neuroscience* (pp. 119–148). Springer-Nature.
43. Gonzalez, J. M. (2006). The power of songs: Why and how does music improve language learning? In C. P. Pascual (Ed.), *Revisiting language learning resources* (pp. 323–346). Cambridge University Press.
44. Legg, R. (2009). Using music to accelerate language learning: An experimental study. *Research in Education, 82*, 1–12.
45. Rainey, D. W., & Larsen, J. D. (2002). The effect of familiar melodies on initial learning and long-term memory for unconnected text. *Music Perception: An Interdisciplinary Journal, 20*(2), 173–186.
46. Calvert, S. L., & Billingsley, R. L. (1998). Young children's recitation and comprehension of information presented by songs. *Journal of Applied Developmental Psychology, 19*(1), 97–108.
47. Calvert, S. L., & Tart, M. (1993). Song versus verbal forms for very-long-term, long-term, and short-term verbatim recall. *Journal of Applied Developmental Psychology, 14*(2), 245–260.
48. Chazin, S., & Neuschatz, J. S. (1990). Using a mnemonic to aid in the recall of unfamiliar information. *Perceptual and Motor Skills, 71*, 1067–1071.
49. Wallace, W. T. (1994). Memory for music: Effect of melody on recall of text. *Journal of Experimental Psychology: Learning, Memory, and Cognition, 20*(6), 1471–1485.
50. Abbott, M. (2002). Using music to promote L2 learning among adult learners. *TESOL Journal, 11*(1), 10–17.
51. Reiterer, S. (2010). The cognitive neuroscience of second language acquisition and bilingualism. In M. Kail & M. Hickmann (Eds.), *Language acquisition across linguistic and cognitive systems* (pp. 307–321). John Benjamins.
52. Peretz, I., Radeau, M., & Arguin, M. (2004). Two-way interactions between music and language: Evidence from priming recognition of tune and lyrics in familiar songs. *Memory & Cognition, 32*(1), 142–152.
53. Cavus, N., & Ibrahim, D. (2009). M-learning: An experiment in using SMS to support learning new English language words. *British Journal of Educational Technology, 40*, 78–91.
54. Wesche, M., & Paribakht, T. S. (2010). *Lexical inferencing in a first and second language*. Multilingual Matters.
55. Chun, D. M., & Plass, J. L. (1996). Effects of multimedia annotations on vocabulary acquisition. *The Modern Language Journal, 80*, 183–198.
56. Hulstijn, J. H., Hollander, M., & Greidanus, T. (1996). Incidental vocabulary learning by advanced foreign language students: The influence of marginal glosses, dictionary use, and reoccurrence of unknown words. *Modern Language Journal, 80*, 327–339.
57. Hulstijn, J. H., & Laufer, B. (1998). What leads to better incidental vocabulary learning: Comprehensible input or comprehensible output? In *Third pacific second language research forum*, Tokyo, Japan, 26–29 March 1998.

58. Hulstijn, J. H., & Trompetter, P. (1999). Incidental learning of second-language vocabulary in computer-assisted reading and writing tasks. In D. Albrechtsen, B. Henrikse, I. M. Mees, & E. Poulsen (Eds.), *Perspectives on foreign and second language pedagogy* (pp. 191–200). Odense University Press.
59. Knight, S. (1994). Dictionary: The tool of last resort in foreign language reading? A new perspective. *Modern Language Journal, 78*, 285–299.
60. Min, H. (2008). EFL vocabulary acquisition and retention reading plus vocabulary enhancement activities and narrow reading. *Language Learning, 58*(1), 73–115.
61. Paribakht, T. S., & Wesche, M. (1997). Vocabulary enhancement activities and reading for meaning in second language vocabulary acquisition. In J. Coady & T. Huckin (Eds.), *Second language vocabulary acquisition: A rationale for pedagogy* (pp. 174–199). Cambridge University Press.
62. Watanabe, Y. (1997). Input, intake, and retention: Effects of increased processing on incidental learning of foreign language vocabulary. *Studies in Second Language Acquisition, 19*, 287–307.
63. Wesche, M., & Paribakht, T. S. (1998). The influence of task in reading-based vocabulary acquisition: Evidence from introspective studies. In K. Haastrup & Å. Viberg (Eds.), *Perspectives on lexical acquisition in a second language* (pp. 19–59). Lund University Press.
64. Wesche, M., & Paribakht, T. S. (2000). Reading-based exercises in second language vocabulary learning: An introspective study. *The Modern Language Journal, 84*, 196–213.
65. Hayes, D. J. (2011). *Assessing vocabulary in context using graduated prompting* (Doctoral dissertation). Retrieved from https://etd.ohiolink.edu/pg_10?0::NO:10:P10_ETD_SUBID:83961
66. Day, R., Omura, C., & Hiramatsu, M. (1991). Incidental EFL vocabulary learning and reading. *Reading in a Foreign Language, 7*(2), 541–551.
67. Dupuy, B., & Krashen, S. (1993). Incidental vocabulary acquisition in French as a foreign language. *Applied Language Learning, 4*, 55–64.
68. Horst, M., Cobb, T., & Meara, P. (1998). Beyond a clockwork orange: Acquiring second language vocabulary through reading. *Reading in a Foreign Language, 11*(2), 207–223.
69. Hulstijn, J. (1992). Retention of inferred and given word meanings: Experiments in incidental vocabulary learning. In P. J. L. Arnaud & H. Bejoing (Eds.), *Vocabulary and applied linguistics* (pp. 113–125). Macmillan.
70. Pitts, M., White, H., & Krashen, S. (1989). Acquiring second language vocabulary through reading: A replication of the Clockwork Orange study using second language acquirers. *Reading in a Foreign Language, 5*(2), 271–275.
71. Waring, R., & Takaki, M. (2003). At what rate do learners learn and retain new vocabulary from reading a graded reader? *Reading in a Foreign Language, 15*, 130–163.
72. Zahar, R., Cobb, T., & Spada, N. (2001). Acquiring vocabulary through reading: Effects of frequency and contextual richness. *The Canadian Modern Language Review, 57*, 541–572.
73. Yamada, M., Kitamura, S., Matsukawa, H., Misono, T., Kitani, N., & Yamauchi, Y. (2014). Collaborative filtering for expansion of learner's background knowledge in online language learning: Does "top-down" processing improve vocabulary proficiency? *Educational Technology Research and Development*. https://doi.org/10.1007/s11423-014-9344-7
74. Jamali Kivi, P., Namaziandost, E., Fakhri Alamdari, E., Ryafikovna Saenko, N., Inga-Arias, M., Fuster-Guillén, D., et al. (2021). The comparative effects of teacher versus peer-scaffolding on EFL learners' incidental vocabulary learning and reading comprehension: A socio-cultural perspective. *Journal of Psycholinguistic Research*. https://doi.org/10.1007/s10936-021-09800-4
75. Ping, A. M., Baranovich, D. L., Manueli, M. K., & Siraj, S. (2014). Promoting self-regulation in vocabulary learning among Chinese EFL learners: A needs analysis. *The Asia-Pacific Education Researcher*. https://doi.org/10.1007/s40299-013-0166-x
76. Chlapana, E., & Tafa, E. (2014). Effective practices to enhance immigrant kindergarteners' second language vocabulary learning through storybook reading. *Reading and Writing*. https://doi.org/10.1007/s11145-014-9510-7

77. Alahmadi, A., & Foltz, A. (2020). Effects of language skills and strategy use on vocabulary learning through lexical translation and inferencing. *Journal of Psycholinguistic Research*. https://doi.org/10.1007/s10936-020-09720-9
78. Yousefi, M. H., & Biria, R. (2018). The effectiveness of L2 vocabulary instruction: A meta-analysis. *Asian-Pacific Journal of Second and Foreign Language Education*. https://doi.org/10.1186/s40862-018-0062-2
79. Chen, I.-S. J. (2020). Music as a mnemonic device for foreign vocabulary learning. *English Teaching & Learning*. https://doi.org/10.1007/s42321-020-00049-z
80. Hasegawa, T., Koshino, M., & Ban, H. (2015). An English vocabulary learning support system for the learner's sustainable motivation. *Springerplus*. https://doi.org/10.1186/s40064-015-0792-2
81. Bahramlou, K., & Esmaeili, A. (2019). The effects of vocabulary enhancement exercises and group dynamic assessment on word learning through lexical inferencing. *Journal of Psycholinguistic Research*. https://doi.org/10.1007/s10936-019-09638-x
82. Wu, X., Lowyck, J., Sercu, L., & Elen, J. (2012). Vocabulary learning from reading: Examining interactions between task and learner related variables. *European Journal of Psychology of Education*. https://doi.org/10.1007/s10212-012-0113-x

Chapter 4
ICT for Vocabulary Learning

4.1 Machine Generated Summaries

Disclaimer: The summaries in this chapter were generated from Springer Nature publications using extractive AI auto-summarization: An extraction-based summarizer aims to identify the most important sentences of a text using an algorithm and uses those original sentences to create the auto-summary (unlike generative AI). As the constituted sentences are machine selected, they may not fully reflect the body of the work, so we strongly advise that the original content is read and cited. The auto generated summaries were curated by the editor to meet Springer Nature publication standards. To cite this content, please refer to the original papers.

Machine generated keywords: gloss, flashcard, multimedia, glossary, paper, electronic, hypermedia, electronic gloss, glossing, paper flashcard, online, esl, digital, glossary information, mobile.

4.1.1 The Effects of Electronic Glossing Types on Foreign Language Vocabulary Learning: Different Types of Format and Glossary Information [65]

This is a machine-generated summary of:

Lee, Hansol; Lee, Jang Ho: The Effects of Electronic Glossing Types on Foreign Language Vocabulary Learning: Different Types of Format and Glossary Information [65]
Published in: The Asia-Pacific Education Researcher (2014)
Link to original: https://doi.org/10.1007/s40299-014-0204-3

M. Udaya, C. R. Reddy (eds.), *Vocabulary, Corpus and Language Teaching*, https://doi.org/10.1007/978-3-031-45986-3_4

If you want to cite the papers, please refer to the original.
For technical reasons we could not place the page where the original quote is coming from.

Abstract-Summary "This study investigated the effects of three different types of electronic textual glosses, tooltip-type glossing, frame-type glossing, and concordance glossing on foreign language vocabulary learning."

"While the first two glossing types provide the definitions of glossed words, with the only difference being their user interface designs, the third type provides authentic concordance sentences for glossed words."

"The results showed that the intermediate EFL learners were affected not by a difference in terms of glossing formats, but by the type of information provided, with tooltip-type and frame-type glosses bringing about more positive learning outcomes."

"While the three groups all experienced a similar cognitive load, the findings further revealed that the tooltip-type and frame-type groups made greater gains of target vocabulary than their concordance counterpart."

4.1.1.1 Introduction

"The present study was driven by Nation's [1] introduction to the different types of glossing available for enhancing FL vocabulary learning in computer-assisted learning environments."

"Nation [1] and Al-Seghayer's [2] descriptions of different types of glossing have recently engaged the interest of FL vocabulary researchers, with one strand of research examining different glossing formats and another investigating different types of glossary information."

"The aim of the present study is to compare the effects of three different electronic glossing types—namely tooltip-type, frame-type, and concordance glosses—which have attracted increasing attention in recent studies (e.g., Nation [1]; AbuSeileek [3]; Poole [4]), but which have not been compared systematically in one empirical study in terms of their effects on FL vocabulary learning."

4.1.1.2 Literature Review

"While previous studies have uncovered significant evidence in favor of the positive effects of electronic glossing, research inquiries into which glossing format and type of information would facilitate vocabulary acquisition have only recently gained attention from researchers, which will be discussed in what follows."

"In this line of research, Yeung [5] examined the effects of two different glossing formats in a paper-based reading context—(1) an integrated format of glossing where vocabulary definition was given right above the glossed word and (2) a separated format which referred to a list of target words and their definitions given at the end of the text, in terms of the reading comprehension, vocabulary learning, and imposed cognitive load on learners with different FL proficiencies."

"The present study aims to extend Poole's study by exposing learners to authentic concordance sentences, and comparing their effect with the two different formats of glossing mentioned in the previous section."

4.1.1.3 Research Questions

"Hypothesis 1a: The gains of the group assigned to the concordance glossing condition will be lower than those of the groups assigned to the definition-type of glossing conditions."

"Hypothesis 1b: The gains of the group assigned to the tooltip-type glossing will be higher than those of the group assigned to the frame-type glossing. (2) Do EFL adult learners assigned to different glossing types in hypermedia reading environments show differences in their self-perceived amount of cognitive load and in their perception of the usefulness of the respective glossing types they encounter?"

"Hypothesis 2a: In view of their level of English language proficiency, the group assigned to the concordance glossing condition and the other two groups assigned to definition-type glossing will experience a similar amount of cognitive load."

4.1.1.4 Research Design

"Adapting the questionnaire in Yeung [5], the authors developed an online post-reading questionnaire which asked about the participants' perception of the difficulty of the reading text and target vocabulary, which was in turn operationalized as the mental effort (i.e., cognitive load) involved in dealing with them via the respective glossing devices."

"The participants were all given the pre-test of vocabulary, which consisted of 30 words found in the target text."

"The results of a one-way ANOVA on the participants' TOEIC scores and the pre-test of vocabulary did not reach a statistical significance ($F(2, 80) = 0.12$, $p = 0.89$ for TOEIC and $F(2, 80) = 0.23$, $p = 0.79$ for the pre-test), indicating that there was no significant difference among the three groups in their general English proficiency and their knowledge of the target words prior to reading at the outset of the study."

4.1.1.5 Results

"This means that the participants from the three groups did not perform in a parallel manner across the three testing points, and this statistical significance appears to be caused by the fact that the mean score of the CG group on the post-test did not increase as sharply as those of the FG and TG groups."

"Comparisons using a post-hoc test confirmed that the mean scores of the FG and TG groups were significantly higher than that of the CG group, but the difference in the mean scores of the FG and TG groups did not reach statistical significance."

"A similar result was found with the delayed test, with the results of ANOVA again revealing the statistical significance of the differences among the groups ($F(2, 80) = 8.64$, $p = 0.001$)."

4.1.1.6 Discussion and Conclusion

"In light of the general findings from previous glossing research that glossing almost without exception results in better learning than the lack thereof, it can be suggested that the three glossing types in the present study enhanced the participants' vocabulary knowledge."

"Regarding the differences among the three glossing types in the post-test and delayed tests, the results showed that those who read the text with definitions of target vocabulary in tooltip-type and frame-type glosses fared better than those who had to infer the meaning of glossed words from authentic concordance sentences; thus, the authors' hypothesis regarding the relative effectiveness of concordance glossing and definition-based glossing was supported."

"The findings of the present study, along with previous studies that have examined the effects of corpora use (but not in a glossing format) have hinted that providing concordance lines only may not be the most effective route in terms of learning the meaning of target vocabulary."

4.1.2 Multimedia-Assisted Self-Learning Materials: The Benefits of E-flashcards for Vocabulary Learning in Chinese as a Foreign Language [66]

This is a machine-generated summary of:

Li, Jui-Teng; Tong, Fuhui: Multimedia-assisted self-learning materials: the benefits of E-flashcards for vocabulary learning in Chinese as a foreign language [66]
Published in: Reading and Writing (2018)
Link to original: https://doi.org/10.1007/s11145-018-9906-x

If you want to cite the papers, please refer to the original.
For technical reasons we could not place the page where the original quote is coming from.

Abstract-Summary "We examined the effects of E-flashcards and paper flashcards on Chinese vocabulary learning and learning attitudes among students learning Chinese as a foreign language."

"One hundred fourth and fifth grade English-speaking students participated in two groups, E-flashcards (n = 50) and paper flashcards (n = 50), to learn 20 new Chinese words."

"Students who used E-flashcards demonstrated more positive learning attitudes toward Chinese word learning than those who used paper flashcards."

4.1.2.1 Introduction

"E-flashcards (or digital flashcards), one type of multimedia-assisted vocabulary learning material, have been found to positively impact second language (L2) learners' word attainment [6, 7], as well as their learning attitudes [7–10]."

"Little research has been conducted on the difference between paper flashcards and E-flashcards on Chinese word learning and recall when measured by reading and listening tests among elementary English-speaking students."

"To address such limitation, in this current study we: (a) compared the effects of E-flashcards versus paper flashcards on elementary Chinese language learners' word learning and recall as measured by reading and listening tests; (b) discovered learners' attitudes toward the use of E-flashcards on Chinese word learning; and (c) discussed the pedagogy of multimedia-assisted vocabulary learning in the context of Chinese as a foreign language."

"We developed E-flashcards on iPads with three features: (a) audio (the sound of target Chinese words); (b) verbal (the written form of Chinese words); and (c) visual (a corresponding picture), so as to make the materials more accessible to students' Chinese learning."

4.1.2.2 Theoretical Framework

"The framework of this study is derived from the cognitive theory of multimedia learning [11]."

"Mayer [11] defined multimedia learning as the idea that new knowledge can be learned through electronic instructional materials presented in both verbal and visual forms."

"Mayer proposed three assumptions of cognitive theory in multimedia learning: dual channels, limited capacity, and active processing."

"The assumption of limited capacity is that through each channel human beings can process a limited amount of information."

4.1.2.3 Literature Review

"Chuang and Ku [7] and Low et al. [10] reported that Chinese language learners exhibited positive attitudes toward the use of E-flashcards to learn Chinese vocabulary words; moreover, they felt more motivated to concentrate on vocabulary word learning."

"Given the nature of the Chinese language, E-flashcards with multiple modalities (i.e., visual, verbal, and audio) are expected to have a stronger effect on Chinese word learning than do paper flashcards."

"There have been no peer-reviewed studies examining elementary Chinese language learners' attitudes toward technology-enhanced materials such as E-flashcards embedded with audio (the sound of the Chinese words), visual (the picture of the words), and verbal (the written words) support on Chinese word recall as measured by reading and listening tests."

"We created E-flashcards with multiple modalities exclusively for use on iPads; in our study, we explored the effects of these self-learning E-flashcards on Chinese language learners' attitudes, as well as on their Chinese word recall."

4.1.2.4 Method

"Because these 20 target Chinese words were identified as unfamiliar words to all students, pre-test scores of two groups (e-flashcard and paper flashcard) were not statistically different from one another for both reading $t(98) = .218$, $p > .05$, and listening $t(98) = .883$, $p > .05$."

"On the first Friday, 25 fourth graders received a set of 20 E-flashcards and self-learned the 20 target words; the other 25 fourth graders received a set of 20 paper flashcards with the same 20 words."

"On the second Friday, 25 fifth graders received a set of 20 E-flashcards and self-learned the 20 target words which were different from the words the fourth graders learned."

"No teacher-led vocabulary instruction was given to the participants, and students were encouraged to pronounce each target word while they used E-flashcards and paper flashcards."

"Students began using E-flashcards to learn words."

"Students began using flashcards to learn words."

4.1.2.5 Results

"Post-hoc comparison revealed that students in E-flashcard group statistically outperformed students in paper flashcard group on the immediate post-test, $F(1, 98) = 51.946$, $p < .01$, Cohen's $d = 1.44$."

"Regarding within-subject effect of test occasion on both E-flashcard approach and paper flashcard approaches, post hoc test showed that students' vocabulary scores were the highest on immediate post-test, followed by on 1-week delayed test, and pre-test."

"Post-hoc comparison revealed that students in E-flashcard group statistically outperformed students in paper flashcard group on the immediate post-test, $F(1, 98) = 543.017$, $p < .01$, Cohen's $d = 4.6$, as well as on the 1-week delayed test, $F(1, 98) = 96.795$, $p < .01$, Cohen's $d = 1.94$."

"The third research question was to discover if there was a significant difference between the use of E-flashcards and paper flashcards on students' attitudes toward Chinese vocabulary word learning."

4.1.2.6 Discussion

"The purpose of this study was to explore the effects of self-learning E-flashcards and paper flashcards on Chinese language learners' Chinese word learning and recall, as well as their learning attitudes."

"We found that compared to novice Chinese language learners who used paper flashcards, learners who used E-flashcards demonstrated higher levels of attention, relevance, confidence, and satisfaction in Chinese word learning."

"Further, E-flashcards with multiple inputs provided the students with more opportunities to explore useful and meaningful information, which assisted them in learning and memorizing Chinese words."

"Given the limited prior research about E-flashcards on Chinese word learning, this study contributes to the field by providing empirical evidence on the integration of paper flashcards with multimedia sources to create E-flashcards and to address learners' attitudes in learning Chinese as a foreign language among elementary English-speaking students."

4.1.2.7 Limitations and Future Directions

"The participants were fourth and fifth grade native English speakers; therefore, results of this study cannot be generalized beyond the grade level of students who are novice Chinese language learners."

"The use of iPads could be a confounding variable on students' learning attitudes as they are generally interested in the device."

"Further, given the purpose of this study which is to investigate how self-learning Chinese word flashcards can be made to be more meaningful and accessible through the use of multimedia to young Chinese language learners, we did not focus on the comparison between the modality."

"We are currently conducting a study to compare students' Chinese word learning between groups with and without the audio input on iPads."

4.1.3 *The Effects of Online Glossary Quizzes and Student Autonomy on Domain Vocabulary Learning in Business Law [67]*

This is a machine-generated summary of:

Lee, Eunbae; Harris, R. Lainie Wilson: The effects of online glossary quizzes and student autonomy on domain vocabulary learning in business law [67]
Published in: Journal of Computing in Higher Education (2018)
Link to original: https://doi.org/10.1007/s12528-018-9183-3

If you want to cite the papers, please refer to the original.
For technical reasons we could not place the page where the original quote is coming from.

Abstract-Summary "Undergraduate business law students (n = 209) took weekly online glossary quizzes via a learning management system before coming to the class."

"Students were divided into two groups where (a) glossary quizzes were required and graded and (b) optional and not graded."

"While both groups valued the glossary quiz as a helpful learning activity, students in the required group made more attempts at quizzes ($t = 17.029$, $p < .01$), received higher scores ($t = 2.841$, $p < .01$), and demonstrated higher perceived competence ($t = 5.544$, $p < .01$) in their command of vocabularies than students in the optional group."

"Findings suggest required glossary quizzes enhance student engagement with quizzes and further improves content learning."

"The use of glossary quizzes proved effective only when students actually completed these numerous times."

"Educators are recommended to encourage repeated attempts at glossary quizzes where unfamiliar vocabularies are crucial to content understanding and professional practice."

4.1.3.1 Introduction

"The goal of teaching the domain specific terminology is two-fold: first, it provides students with a foundational understanding of the discipline."

"Domain specific vocabularies are also an important part of college coursework because these offer a primary source of the nature and distinct characteristics of the discipline."

"In Business Law, discipline-specific vocabularies introduced in content areas often have many of these everyday meanings that may distract and confuse students [12]."

"It is important to understand the relationship between the competency of discipline-specific vocabulary and overall performance on the subject in order to adequately support students in its mastery."

"This study sheds light on the impact learning domain vocabularies using online glossary quizzes may have on student academic performance and engagement in the context of Business Law."

"This study informs the role of autonomy and perceived competence in student engagement with glossary quizzes, and its extended effect on student academic performance."

4.1.3.2 Theoretical Framework

"Self-determination theory suggests that humans have innate needs of autonomy and perceived competence [13]."

"Autonomy, when applied to learning, is defined as a perceived control over learning environments: what, when, where, and how students will engage in learning activities and how their needs and interests are respected by instructors and other stakeholders [14]."

"Perceived competence refers to student beliefs about their ability to do well in an academic environment [15]."

"In the context of jargon-heavy disciplines, perceived competence is particularly important because perceived competence in language proficiency is reportedly a significant predictor of performance and engagement with the academic tasks [16]."

"In language learning settings, instructional activities should be designed with research based evidence to foster a student's innate need for perceived autonomy and competence, capturing the learner's desire to succeed despite growing levels of difficulty [17]."

4.1.3.3 Literature Review

"In stage five, advanced language proficiency students have knowledge of some specialized vocabulary and can speak [the second language] comparable to same-age native speakers [18]."

"The teacher bore all responsibility for educating students in the classroom, but Yang [18] suggests the student and teacher should share this responsibility in a second language learning classroom."

"In a Turkish university where courses were conducted in English, their non-native language, students' perceived competence in their English language proficiency was a significant predictor of academic performance and engagement with academic tasks [16]."

"Previous research suggested that students' autonomous motivation and perceived competence affect student engagement and performances [13]."

"Little is known about the connection between students' autonomous academic motivation and content language learning, particularly when supported by online glossary quiz."

"This study examines the role of autonomy and perceived competence in student performance on and engagement with the glossary quiz."

4.1.3.4 Methods

"After the course ended, glossary quiz scores, the number of attempts at each quiz, and final grade were collected."

"In both groups, students took weekly glossary quizzes online through the university's learning management system at their convenience."

"After the course ended, the followings are collected: the glossary quiz scores, the number of attempts at each quiz, and final course grades."

"The presurvey served three purposes: (1) it solicited demographic information of the participants, (2) it assessed participant's initial perceived competence in their command of terms and definitions using a Perceived Competence for Learning (PCL), and (3) it identified student motivation to enroll in the course using the Learning Self-Regulation Questionnaire (LSRQ)."

"IMI jointly assessed students' levels of engagement in the areas of enjoyment/interest, effort, perceived choice, value/usefulness, and perceived competence on the glossary quizzes."

"Postsurvey also included open-ended questions on whether students would recommend future students make use of course glossary quizzes."

4.1.3.5 Findings

"It appeared that the required group exhibited more autonomous motivation overall shown in IMI scores while the optional group perceived slightly higher choice in taking the glossary quizzes shown in LSRQ scores."

"The two groups significantly differed in their engagement ($t = 3.306$, $p < .01$) with the glossary quizzes in the areas of perceived competence ($t = 5.544$, $p < .01$), enjoyment ($t = 3.636$, $p < .01$), and effort ($t = 3.341$, $p < .01$)."

"When asked why they would recommend taking the glossary quiz to future students, among 29 respondents of the required group, 20 stated the helpful aspect of the quizzes and seven recommended quizzes only for the grade, and two mentioned both the grade and helpfulness."

"No statistical significance was observed between students' final grade or quiz performances and whether students viewed the glossary quizzes positively or negatively."

4.1.3.6 Discussion

"Even though final course grades were not significantly different between the groups, there was merit in requiring glossary quizzes in terms of student competence in legal terms and engagement with the glossary tool."

"While the glossary quizzes in our study were generally well-received by students and described as being helpful for learning in the course, there was still a lack of a strong statistical correlation between use of the quizzes and improved overall grades."

"The autonomy support scores collected in this study (shown in LCQ) indicated that while the instructor's interaction with students remained consistent across the groups, having the option to take or not take glossary quizzes was not interpreted as autonomy support."

"While perceived competence played a significant role in students engaging with the glossary quizzes, it did not lead to high course grades."

4.1.3.7 Implications and Conclusion

"This study was conducted in order to learn how to better help students master terms necessary for grasping the concepts of business law We also examined the role of autonomy and perceived competence in students' engagement with glossary quizzes and the relationship between interaction with quizzes and overall course performance."

"Encouraging students to see the real world value of academic tasks beyond the classroom assessment enhances student autonomous motivation and engagement."

"Helping students set personalized goals for task completion and follow through can help students more actively engage in the language-learning academic tasks [17]."

"Student engagement with domain-specific terms isolated from a real world context may not have the desired instructional impact."

"The review of student comments noted that many students would encourage future classmates to utilize glossary quizzes for the exact reason these were created: because quizzes were helpful in understanding the material."

4.1.4 Augmented Reality as Multimedia: The Case for Situated Vocabulary Learning [68]

This is a machine-generated summary of:

Santos, Marc Ericson C.; Lübke, Arno in Wolde; Taketomi, Takafumi; Yamamoto, Goshiro; Rodrigo, Ma. Mercedes T.; Sandor, Christian; Kato, Hirokazu: Augmented reality as multimedia: the case for situated vocabulary learning [68]
Published in: Research and Practice in Technology Enhanced Learning (2016)
Link to original: https://doi.org/10.1186/s41039-016-0028-2

If you want to cite the papers, please refer to the original.
For technical reasons we could not place the page where the original quote is coming from.

Abstract-Summary "We treat AR as a type of multimedia that is situated in authentic environments and apply multimedia learning theory as a framework for developing our educational applications."

"We share our experiences in developing a handheld AR system and one specific use case, namely, situated vocabulary learning."

"Results of our evaluations show that we are able to create AR applications with good system usability."

4.1.4.1 Introduction

"Few research works have been conducted to substantiate AR's benefits to learning [19]."

"Dede [20] explains that AR is useful for supporting ubiquitous learning in authentic environments."

"The role of AR in ubiquitous learning is to present the information onto the real environment thereby creating a stronger connection between the digital content and the real environment."

"In a review conducted in 2013, Santos et al. [21] found only seven research articles reporting evidence of AR's effectiveness in improving learning outcomes."

"We apply AR to the task of memorizing vocabulary words and test AR's effect on both learning and student motivation."

"Because there is little literature substantiating the benefits of AR to learning, we test AR's effectiveness as a platform for a memorization task and examine its impact on student motivation."

4.1.4.2 Augmented Reality for Learning

"People use some AR browsers to see virtual labels and symbols integrated with a live video feed of the real environment."

"One important work is Construct3D [22, 23] which uses AR to teach students mathematics and geometry concepts."

"Although Construct3D take advantage of embodied cognition and collaborative learning, these applications do not use AR for displaying the relationship of the virtual contents to the real environment."

"In our work, we exploit such AR features by teaching vocabulary through the relationship between virtual objects and the real environment."

"AR running on handheld devices can be used for displaying content in big environments."

"Billinghurst and Duenser [24] call for more interdisciplinary research to ground AR applications in learning theories."

"For our experiments, we designed AR applications for learning Filipino and German words by applying the principles of multimedia learning theory [25] and its related research."

4.1.4.3 Vocabulary Learning Systems

"Context is important to vocabulary learning because students can use it for forming stronger associations between the new word and the objects in the real world [26]."

"Researchers have used personalized learning systems that tailor-fit the vocabulary content to students' internal context, i.e., their current level of competence [27]."

"Systems for situated vocabulary learning take advantage of situated cognition by selecting words that are associated with the environment and teaching only the words that are useful."

"In situated vocabulary learning, the words are learned in the context of its use thus facilitating knowledge transfer."

"Aside from presenting information related to the user's current environment, the tagged added learning object (TANGO) system uses RFID to tag the objects in the environment to present vocabulary words relevant to an object."

"The most important feature of situated vocabulary learning is the presentation of useful vocabulary words relevant to the current environment."

4.1.4.4 Multimedia Learning Applied to Augmented Reality

"Learning only takes place if the learner actively processes incoming information by connecting it to prior knowledge."

"Integrating information with prior knowledge Situated vocabulary learning leverages on the prior knowledge of places."

"Situated multimedia aids in the cognitive process of integrating incoming information with prior knowledge."

"In the case of AR, the environment is a given and authors of AR learning contents must make use of the environment creatively."

"They did not find any significant differences in vocabulary recognition nor in any interaction between multimedia modes and learning style preferences of the students."

"Based on these works, we implemented features in our AR system that allow users to access text, audio, and pictures during the learning scenario."

"In a separate study with 121 senior high school students, Lin and Hsiao [28] studied the effects of the use of still images against simple animations in vocabulary learning."

4.1.4.5 Practical Considerations in Applying Augmented Reality

"Cuendet et al. [29] shares five design principles for adopting AR for classroom use."

"The five design principles are integrating AR to other class activities, empowering the teacher, providing the teacher awareness of the state of students, flexibility to adapt the activities to evolving scenarios, and minimizing functionalities to what is required at a given time."

"Based on a survey with teachers and students in Malaysia, Sumadio and Rambli [30] observed that although most of them experienced AR for the first time, they perceived that the demonstrations presented to them are useful for educational practice."

"Teachers and students expressed that bringing AR to educational use would make the learning process more enjoyable."

"Based on interviews with teachers in the Philippines [31, 32], AR is perceived to be useful because it offers learning by experiencing some activity that cannot be done now in the classroom."

4.1.4.6 Design Goals

"What we discussed so far, we list the following design goals based on multimedia learning, past works on situated vocabulary learning, and some practical considerations for future adoption to educational settings: 1."

"Support cognitive processes of selecting, organizing, and integrating information 3."

"Allow interactions with the environment and objects in the environment 4."
"Present multimodal information, namely, texts, images, and sounds 5."

4.1.4.7 System Design and Implementation

"We created a handheld AR system that can display any combination of multimedia including image, animation, sound, and text on a real environment."

"We accomplished this by simply filling the handheld AR system with content for the situated vocabulary learning of Filipino and German words."

"The Controller receives the marker ID and camera view matrix from the Tracker and uses these information to specify the behavior of the on-screen display."

"Fiducial markers in the video feed were located using the ARToolKit, which also outputs the marker's ID and the matrix representing the current view of the camera."

"The images are transformed depending on the camera view and are inserted in the video feed to suggest 3D registration, that is, to give an impression that the graphics co-exist with the real objects."

"We used the AR system to construct two situated vocabulary learning systems: one for 30 Filipino words and the other for 10 German words."

4.1.4.8 User Studies

"We compared the AR applications to a non-AR version which is a tablet application that mimics flash card interaction."

"Advising the students who use the AR application to view all the content several times will interrupt their natural learning style."

"Students will perform worse on a delayed post-test with non-AR compared with the immediate post-test."

"Students will perform worse on a delayed post-test with AR compared with the immediate post-test."

"Students will perform better in an immediate post-test with non-AR."

"Students will perform better in a delayed post-test with AR."

"Both AR and non-AR applications logged time-stamped button pushes, words studied, and tablet acceleration and orientation based on the built-in sensors."

"We adapted a within-subjects design with 14 participants (8 male, 6 female, aged 17–20, Filipino undergraduate students) to test the application for learning 20 German words (10 for AR and 10 for non-AR)."

4.1.4.9 Results and Discussion

"We observed significant decrease in immediate to delayed post-test scores with non-AR but not for AR, suggesting that students who learned via AR retained more vocabulary."

"No significant differences were observed in learning outcomes between using AR and non-AR applications for vocabulary learning."

"In the immediate post-test, the non-AR group scored significantly higher with a moderate effect (d = 0.75) compared with the AR group, thus supporting hypothesis 3."

"That implementation quality was a factor affecting the learning of the students, we could do fairer comparisons of post-test scores if both AR and non-AR applications have almost the same SUS score."

"Marginally significant differences were observed in the test scores of AR and non-AR groups for the immediate post-tests."

"There was no significant difference between the recognition test between using AR (M = 94%, SD = 8%) and using non-AR (M = 95%, SD = 8%) for vocabulary learning."

4.1.4.10 Conclusions

"In our work, we discussed our experience in developing and evaluating an AR application for learning experiences based on an authentic environment."

"As a use case of the AR system, we filled the system with Filipino and German vocabulary contents, thereby creating two AR applications for situated vocabulary learning."

"We observed differences in immediate post-tests wherein students who used the non-AR application performed better than those who used AR."

"We observed a larger difference between immediate post-test and delayed post-test for the students who used the non-AR application."

"Aside from differences in post-tests, the potential of AR lies in the difference in the learning experience, more specifically, reducing cognitive load, improving attention, and increasing satisfaction."

"For future work, experiments with bigger sample size must be used to explore deeper into how students can learn better with AR."

4.1.5 Effects of Multimedia Annotations on Incidental Vocabulary Learning and Reading Comprehension of Advanced Learners of English as a Foreign Language [69]

This is a machine-generated summary of:

Akbulut, Yavuz: Effects of multimedia annotations on incidental vocabulary learning and reading comprehension of advanced learners of english as a foreign language [69]
Published in: Instructional Science (2007)

Link to original: https://doi.org/10.1007/s11251-007-9016-7

If you want to cite the papers, please refer to the original.
For technical reasons we could not place the page where the original quote is coming from.

Abstract-Summary "The study investigates immediate and delayed effects of different hypermedia glosses on incidental vocabulary learning and reading comprehension of advanced foreign language learners."

"The data were collected through a vocabulary pre-test, a vocabulary post-test, a delayed vocabulary test as well as a reading comprehension test."

"No differences were observed on the reading comprehension test."

"The qualitative data revealed that hypermedia reading had positive impact on participants' attitudes towards foreign language reading and vocabulary learning."

4.1.5.1 Introduction

"These applications provide tools to incorporate glosses into authentic texts, thus making them more comprehensible for L2 learners and facilitating learning new words while the focus is on reading, i.e., incidental vocabulary learning."

"Since glosses in a hypermedia environment can be provided not only in the form of text, but also audio, picture, video, and sound, it has become crucial to investigate whether multimodal glosses or annotations are effective in facilitating reading comprehension and vocabulary learning."

"The present study explores the effects of multimedia annotations, particularly pictures and videos, on vocabulary learning and reading comprehension of advanced learners of English as a foreign language."

"These studies suggest that multimedia annotations with word definitions and visuals (e.g., pictures and videos) help learners learn vocabulary more efficiently than annotations with word definitions alone."

4.1.5.2 Experimental Design

"A hardcopy version of the original text was piloted with 20 senior students who did not participate in the original study in order to determine the words to be annotated."

"This test included a checklist in which students were asked to indicate the words they remembered from the text."

"The first section of the test took 6.5 min to complete in the pilot group, so the time on task was determined as 7 min."

"In the pilot study, junior students were asked to read the hardcopy version of the text, since the development of the software was not completed yet."

"The pilot group, 22 junior students, completed the test in 14 min."

"Eleven days before the administration of the software, students were given two sections of the vocabulary test (i.e., meaning recognition and meaning production)."

4.1.5.3 Results

"In order to determine whether these differences were statistically significant, a 3 (Annotation type) × 2 (Time: Post-test and delayed post-test) mixed-design ANOVA was conducted."

"In order to determine whether these differences were statistically significant, a 3 (Annotation type) × 3 (Time: Pre-test, post-test, and delayed post-test) mixed-design ANOVA was conducted."

"The interaction between time and annotation type was significant on the immediate post-test ($F_{Immediate} = 4.797$, $p < .01$); the video group got the highest scores, the picture group ranked second and the definition group got the lowest scores."

"To determine whether these differences were statistically significant, a 3 (Annotation type) × 3 (Time: Pre-test, post-test, and delayed post-test) mixed design ANOVA was conducted."

"The interaction between time and annotation type was significant on both the immediate and delayed post-tests ($F_{Immediate} = 7.022$, $p < .002$; $F_{Delayed} = 12.318$, $p < .001$)."

4.1.5.4 Discussion

"Findings of the study suggest that combining definitions of words with associated visuals regardless of the type of visual used is more effective in facilitating vocabulary learning than providing only definitions of words."

"The availability of visual annotations along with word meanings helped L2 learners perform better on vocabulary tests than a single type of textual annotation."

"As for L2 reading comprehension, the results of this study confirm Ariew and Erçetin's [33] findings, which suggested no relationship between annotation use and reading comprehension for advanced L2 learners."

"This study provided evidence for facilitative effects of multimedia annotations for L2 incidental vocabulary learning."

"Findings of the study suggest important pedagogical implications for the use of hypermedia in L2 vocabulary learning and reading."

"The qualitative data suggested that subjects found hypermedia highly useful for their reading comprehension and vocabulary learning regardless of the type of annotation they were exposed to."

4.1.5.5 Limitations and Suggestions for Further Research

"The target population of the study consisted of advanced level language learners attending an English-medium Turkish university to learn English for academic purposes."

"This study should be replicated in other learning contexts with students from different proficiency levels to generalize findings to a larger target population and to different learning environments."

"The results cannot be generalized to people who are not pre-tested."

"In order to eliminate the interaction of pre-testing and the experimental instrument, a Solomon Four-group Design may be employed in a further study."

"Employing on-screen tests where visual elements are incorporated would be more suitable for use in hypermedia environments."

"Besides, reading and vocabulary learning strategies employed at different proficiency levels should be examined."

4.1.6 Evaluation of Electronic and Paper Textual Glosses on Second Language Vocabulary Learning and Reading Comprehension [70]

This is a machine-generated summary of:

Lee, Ho; Lee, Hansol; Lee, Jang Ho: Evaluation of Electronic and Paper Textual Glosses on Second Language Vocabulary Learning and Reading Comprehension [70]

Published in: The Asia-Pacific Education Researcher (2015)
Link to original: https://doi.org/10.1007/s40299-015-0270-1

If you want to cite the papers, please refer to the original.

For technical reasons we could not place the page where the original quote is coming from.

Abstract-Summary "We examined the effectiveness of electronic and paper textual glosses on second language vocabulary learning and reading comprehension within a cognitive load theory framework."

"We adopted an experimental design using Korean undergraduate learners of English as a foreign language, who read a target text under one of the three reading conditions: electronic gloss, paper gloss, and no gloss."

"The results showed that the electronic glossing condition resulted in the greatest gains of vocabulary."

"The electronic glossing condition was also the most efficient in light of the cognitive load framework, showing the highest instructional efficiency."

4.1.6.1 Introduction

"Glossing, an instructional method of providing meaning for a selected word in a text, has gained much attention from researchers in the field of second language (L2) studies (e.g., Hulstijn et al. [35]; Jacobs et al. [36])."

"Studies regarding the relative effects of electronic glosses and their pen-and-paper counterpart (paper glosses, henceforth) are rare."

"Electronic glosses have not yet been shown to be more effective than paper glosses."

"In light of this gap, in the present study we compared the effects of electronic and paper glosses on vocabulary learning and reading comprehension in a sample of Korean learners of English as a Foreign Language (EFL) at the university level using an experimental design."

4.1.6.2 Study Background

"A review of the literature on glossing in L2 reading shows that providing glossary information for target words contributes to vocabulary learning, whereas it may not enhance L2 reading comprehension."

"We propose a more comprehensive methodology, recruiting intermediate-level L2 learners (the largest group across proficiency levels), investigating reading comprehension and vocabulary acquisition, including target lexical items (TLIs) selected from a wide range of frequency bands (e.g., TLIs fell between the first 5 and 10 k word families, most of which were not familiar to our participants), and providing L2 definitions as glossary information (e.g., intermediate-level L2 learners are not expected to have comprehension problems with L2 glosses; Nation [34])."

"Yeung [5] administered seven-point Likert scale items regarding participants' perception of difficulty of target vocabulary in printed paper reading contexts, and compared the effect of two different glossing formats on reading comprehension and vocabulary learning."

4.1.6.3 Methods

"After replacing some of the words in the original passage with low-frequency words, we gave a vocabulary test consisting of 50 lexical items drawn from the target text to eight students who had similar profiles to those in the main study."

"The reading comprehension test consisted of ten multiple choice items, with the questions assessing whether test-takers accurately understood the information described in the target text or not."

"At the outset of the study, the participants were given a vocabulary pre-test, which consisted of 30 English lexical items from the target reading text."

"Of this pre-test, ten lexical items that were found to be unfamiliar to more than 90% of the participants were selected as the final set of target lexical items to be glossed in the present study, because no lexical items were unknown to the entire group of participants."

4.1.6.4 Results

"Simple regression analysis showed that the differences among the three groups for reading comprehension test scores did not reach statistical significance ($b = 0.44$, $p > 0.10$)."

"These findings indicate that the differences in reading conditions did not lead to any significant differences in reading when the density rate of unfamiliar words in the target text was low (approximately 5%)."

"All groups made significant gains on the post-test, which was taken immediately after the reading activity, and these gains were retained for another 2 weeks."

"The results of one-way ANOVA showed that there were significant effects of reading conditions in terms of instructional efficiency, both for the post-test $F(2, 75) = 4.80$, $p < 0.05$ and for the delayed test, $F(2, 75) = 4.12$, $p < 0.05$."

4.1.6.5 Discussion and Conclusion

"With regard to vocabulary learning, the participants in the electronic glossing condition group fared better than the paper-based glossing group as well as the control group, and this difference was maintained 2 weeks after the reading task."

"Based on our findings, we suggest that the participants in the present study, who were reportedly competent users of computers and intermediate-level L2 learners, adapted well to computer-assisted reading environments and benefited from the electronic glosses therein."

"It is possible that the three reading conditions examined in this study may bring about differences in learning other aspects of vocabulary knowledge (e.g., form), and this question should be explored in future research."

"Another line of research that is worth considering is the effects of electronic glosses and computer-assisted environments on learners with different levels of computer literacy and different amounts of experience with electronic glossing and computer-assisted reading."

4.1.7 Self-Directed Learning of Core Vocabulary in English by EFL Learners: Comparing the Outcomes from Paper and Mobile Application Flashcards [71]

This is a machine-generated summary of:

Xodabande, Ismail; Pourhassan, Asqar (Aydin); Valizadeh, Mohammadreza: Self-directed learning of core vocabulary in English by EFL learners: comparing the outcomes from paper and mobile application flashcards [71]
Published in: Journal of Computers in Education (2021)
Link to original: https://doi.org/10.1007/s40692-021-00197-6

If you want to cite the papers, please refer to the original.
For technical reasons we could not place the page where the original quote is coming from.

Abstract-Summary "Within this line of inquiry, the current study explored vocabulary learning outcomes from paper and mobile application flashcards."

"The study used a repeated measures design, by exposing the participants (55 high-school students) to different learning conditions and testing their receptive knowledge of core vocabulary in English in three junctures of time over a year."

"The participants were asked to use digital or paper flashcards for vocabulary learning, and two standard measures of vocabulary knowledge in pre- and post-tests were used to compare vocabulary gains."

"The findings underscore the long-term impacts of mobile-assisted vocabulary learning, and the affordances provided by such platforms for learning a considerable number of words by EFL learners."

4.1.7.1 Introduction

"Although research investigating the use of various mobile applications for language and vocabulary learning is gaining increased attention, most studies were conducted in short-term interventions which makes it difficult to understand long-term impacts of mobile devices on language development [37, 38]."

"The current study aimed to fill part of this gap and investigated the long-term impacts of using a mobile phone flashcard application (i.e., Lexilize) and traditional paper flashcards on vocabulary learning of 55 EFL high-school students over a period of 12 months."

"The study adds to the growing body of literature on mobile-assisted vocabulary learning and sheds some light on the affordances provided by flashcard applications for developing vocabulary knowledge among EFL learners."

"By employing these tests, the current study investigated the contribution of mobile-assisted vocabulary learning on second-language knowledge development among EFL learners, which makes it possible to compare the results across different learning contexts."

4.1.7.2 Method

"Based on smartphone device ownership and also participants' preferences for using different materials for learning essential English vocabulary, they were divided into an experimental (N = 36) and a control (N = 19) group."

"In order to learn the items in this vocabulary list, the participants in the control group were given a list of NGSL words and their translations in their first language (L1), and relevant flashcards printed on paper (an English word on the one side and L1 translation on the other side of the cards)."

"This was followed by assigning the participants into the experimental and control groups and giving them different materials for learning core English vocabulary."

"In order to assess the learning gains, receptive vocabulary knowledge of the participants was tested again in six-month intervals using the NGSLT and the different versions of the updated VLT."

4.1.7.3 Results

"As for the pre-tests, the mean values for the scores on NGSLT were 46.56 (SD = 5.07) and 49.16 (SD = 5.19) for the experimental and control groups, respectively."

"Regarding the post-tests, the mean values for the NGSLT were 63.61 (SD = 6.06) and 54.32 (SD = 6.24) for the experimental and control groups."

"With regard to the second post-tests, the experimental group had mean values of 71.64 (SD = 7.56) for scores on NGSLT, and 81.69 (SD = 6.89) for VLT (version A)."

"From the first post-test to the second post-test (time 3), obtained scores on NGSLT followed a similar pattern for both groups, and all participants improved their vocabulary knowledge."

"This indicate significant differences in the scores obtained by the experimental and control groups on NGSLT and VLT measures."

4.1.7.4 Discussion

"The current study provided empirical evidence for the effectiveness of mobile application flashcards in learning core vocabulary in English."

"One reason for the observed differences might be the motivational profile of the learners, as the participants in the current study were highly motivated to improve their English vocabulary, and motivation is among the most important factors that impacts learning outcomes [39–41]."

"The flashcard application used in this study also employed the gaming features that contributed to increased use of the digital flashcards for vocabulary learning."

"This is also in line with previous studies that investigated the contribution of mobile applications for learning essential English vocabulary [42, 43]."

"As the participants of this study learned a considerable number (around 25%) of general service vocabulary over a year, it seems that the use of digital flashcards has a great potential to shortcut this process."

4.1.7.5 Conclusion

"In light of the recent developments in mobile-assisted language learning, the use of mobile applications and digital flashcards for vocabulary learning in gaining increased attention in language education."

"The findings revealed a significant main effect for time in the use of mobile devices for vocabulary learning and pointed the effectiveness of digital flashcards over traditional materials."

"The current study was also an attempt to link the findings from corpus-based study of language and materials development to address the vocabulary learning needs [44]."

"Although vocabulary knowledge entails different components [45, 46], the current study focused only on written receptive knowledge of English words and did not examine how the use of different interventions result in developments in other aspects of vocabulary knowledge such as pronunciation, collocations, etc. Nonetheless, the current study provided empirical evidence for the effectiveness of mobile-assisted vocabulary learning in general, and digital flashcards applications in particular."

4.1.8 Factors Influencing ESL Players' Use of Vocabulary Learning Strategies in Massively Multiplayer Online Role-Playing Games (MMORPG) [72]

This is a machine-generated summary of:

Ng, Lee Luan; Rino Sharieful Azizie, None; Chew, Shin Yi: Factors Influencing ESL Players' Use of Vocabulary Learning Strategies in Massively Multiplayer Online Role-Playing Games (MMORPG) [72]

Published in: The Asia-Pacific Education Researcher (2021)

Link to original: https://doi.org/10.1007/s40299-021-00578-6

Copyright of the summarized publication:

If you want to cite the papers, please refer to the original.
For technical reasons we could not place the page where the original quote is coming from.

Abstract-Summary "The study investigates the impact of Massively Multiplayer Online Role-Playing Game (MMORPG) on players' application of vocabulary learning strategies."

"Apart from identifying the vocabulary learning strategies used by the ESL players during online gaming, in order to find out how aspects related to MMORPG influence the use of strategies, data were also obtained from online semi-structured interviews with these (ESL) players who are involved in Guild Wars 2, a popular MMORPG computer game."

"Using Gu and Johnson's [49] categorisation of vocabulary learning strategies (VLS), it was found that these ESL players utilise metacognitive, cognitive, memory and activation strategies in order to learn game-related vocabulary during the MMORPG game-play sessions."

4.1.8.1 Introduction

"There is insufficient research that have looked into the use of digital games for educational purposes such as for language learning purposes."

"It is also important to explore the potential of digital games for educational purposes as it could pave way for more enhanced and innovative language learning environment for ESL players."

"Despite the growing popularity of MMORPGs, there is still a lack of studies that have explored its potential for learners such as the vocabulary language learning strategies used by gamers during online game-play sessions as they have to understand game instructions that are mostly in English."

"There is a need to investigate how English language learning takes place in online digital gaming platform such as in MMORPGs."

4.1.8.2 Literature Review

"In a study by Mofareh [47] that reviewed the use of technology in English language teaching, the findings revealed that: (a) technology allows students to practice independence in learning language, (b) students actively want to use technology in language learning, and (c) technology aids students to create strong content knowledge wherever they find it."

"Based on the research findings of different VLS used by ESL learners during gameplay sessions, it can be seen that MMORPG can be a potential language learning platform for gamers to create, select and use different vocabulary learning strategies to enhance or develop their own language learning experience [48]."

"In a study that explored the use of vocabulary learning strategies by Chinese English learners in MMORPGs, Bytheway [48] observed that the students had mainly used selective attention and guessing strategies during game-play sessions where they guessed the meanings of words based on pictures or gestures."

4.1.8.3 Methodology

"In order to assess participants' use of vocabulary learning strategies, the online gaming platform Guild Wars 2, a free-to-play MMORPG was selected."

"The researcher also simultaneously used an Open Broadcaster Studio (OBS) software in order to capture video and audio recordings of the 12-h game-play sessions, as well as to conduct semi-structured online interview sessions with the four participants."

"Discord is considered as the main communication tool for the study's online gaming sessions and online interviews as it facilitated the process of communication between the researcher and research participants."

"The researcher had conducted a total of four semi-structured online interviews with each of the four participants individually in a span of 2 weeks after the last game session was conducted."

"Other than applying thematic analysis in investigating the VLS used by the ESL players, the researcher also adopted the categorisation of VLS from Gu and Johnson's [49] framework and mapped the VLS used by participants during the game-play sessions into their respective categories."

4.1.8.4 Results and Discussion

"Based on the data gathered using the OBS software and online interviews, these are four factors that influenced how the learners used vocabulary learning strategies and they consist of; (a) the role of the MMOPG storyline in enhancing gaming immersion, (b) freedom to learn while being away from classroom-related rules, (c) social interaction that enriches players' learning experience, and (d) the role of collaboration among the MMORPG community in enriching players' learning experience."

"Similar to the immersion factor, with the opportunity to simultaneously communicate in online games, players are able to incidentally learn language via communicating with one another."

"The results from interviews with the participants were indicative of the fact that social interaction in the MMORPG community could be effective for ESL players to learn languages."

"P1 mentioned that the engaging environment of MMORPG has enabled her to experience collaborative language learning with other players in the online community."

4.1.8.5 Conclusion

"The findings of the current study have shown that online games can be integrated into contemporary teaching and learning processes as a supplementary option that could enhance students' learning of English language vocabulary."

"The findings also suggest that the interaction during online games promotes authentic communication among players, as they need to communicate effectively in order to achieve their game-related goals."

"Future studies are advised to expand the sample size and incorporate measurement of participants' mastery of vocabulary items using the pre- and post-test methods in order to determine whether there is an improvement in test scores after playing online games."

4.1.9 EmoTan: Enhanced Flashcards for Second Language Vocabulary Learning with Emotional Binaural Narration [73]

This is a machine-generated summary of:

Fukushima, Shogo: EmoTan: enhanced flashcards for second language vocabulary learning with emotional binaural narration [73]
Published in: Research and Practice in Technology Enhanced Learning (2019)
Link to original: https://doi.org/10.1186/s41039-019-0109-0

If you want to cite the papers, please refer to the original.
For technical reasons we could not place the page where the original quote is coming from.

Abstract-Summary "We report on the design and evaluation of a flashcard application, enhanced with emotional binaural narration to support second language (L2) vocabulary learning."

"Enhancing textual flashcards with emotional narration in the learner's native language can foster the retention of new L2 words in episodic rather than semantic memory as greater emotive expression reinforces episodic memory retention."

"We evaluated the effects of binaural emotive narration with traditional textual flashcards on L2 word retention (immediate and delayed) in laboratory experiments with native Japanese-speaking English learners."

4.1.9.1 Introduction

"To learn new English words with these mobile devices, learners generally memorize words while listening to the pronunciation in online dictionaries [50–53] or flashcard applications [54, 55]."

"Released for smartphones and gaming devices, this application allows learners to learn a word through sample sentences and voice."

"The key contributions of the proposed approach are as follows: We designed narrations to memorize English words in the emotionally rich episodic memory and not semantic memory, and we described the method of producing the narration."

"The effectiveness of the narration using flashcard application was evaluated by comparing our method to the traditional pronunciations of English words."

"We show that our proposed method could aid in retaining more English words into long-term memory than traditional pronunciation by applying our method to a general English learning style, in which the learners freely memorize words using a typical flashcard application on a tablet until they are satisfied."

4.1.9.2 Related Work

"To apply the memory retention effect of emotion to vocabulary learning, it is better to use this retention effect not only for emotive words, such as in the study of Kensinger and Corkin [56], but also for non-emotive words."

"An insufficient number of sounds or sound effects exist compared to the size of the English vocabulary, making it difficult to find enough emotional stimuli that match the meaning of English words."

"There has been no methodology introduced yet for applying this binaural emotional technology to English vocabulary learning."

"To acquire vocabulary in long-term memory, it is important to deeply understand the meaning of a word and repetitively learn the word to memorize it."

"We describe a method of producing the audio contents that represent the meaning of the English words and evoke emotion at the same time."

4.1.9.3 Narration Design

"To create impressive emotional narrations, expressive voice actors were adopted as narrators under the supervision of English native speakers (supervisors) with English teaching experience."

"According to their meanings, 100 words were grouped into ten categories: person, emotion, contact, communication, food, object, social, environment, impression, and sound effect."

"In the case of the word "swig" (expression category 1), for example, the background music of a bar is played, with the voice of the actor saying "Cheers!"".

"In the case of the word "prank" (expression category 3), the voice actor approached the listener from behind and said "BOO!""

"In the case of the word "maraud" (expression category 4), the sound effect of an approaching bike was played and the actor stated, "Argh!""

"In the case of the word "grotto" (expression category 6), the sound effect of dripping water in a cave was played along with a voice stating, "Wow!""

4.1.9.4 Prototype Flashcard Application

"A flashcard is a card on which a word is written, depending on its purpose."

"To employ it for introducing English words, English and Japanese word pairs were displayed on the front side, while the narration was played."

"The user can save words and narrations on his/her personal computer in advance and input correspondences between words and sounds using Excel."

"By synchronizing it with Dropbox, words and sounds are displayed on the tablet in a flashcard format."

4.1.9.5 Experiment 1: Memorize Under a Controlled Environment

"The next ten words were learned using the proposed method, and the participants immediately took a memorization test as well."

"The participants first memorized ten English words by the baseline or proposed methods."

"This suggested that the participants were able to memorize and retain more English language words with the proposed method than the baseline method (RQ2)."

"According to a feedback form completed after the delayed test, many positive comments were communicated by the participants: "The retention rate is remarkably different between the actor's voice and the conventional voice"; "I remember the story from the beginning to the end, and I can reproduce the story"; "The actor's voice is remarkably impressive compared to the conventional one, but it might be difficult to completely memorize English word pairs with one memorization"; "I would like to use it for learning English words if the application is released"; "I remembered vividly that the sound source moved from the left to the right of the headphones, and I also remember I felt a chilling sensation at this point."".

4.1.9.6 Experiment 2: Memorize Under a Freeform Learning Environment

"The same participant experienced both the baseline and proposed methods, and we compared the number of words forgotten among the methods."

"The participants first learned ten words by the baseline approach and then performed an immediate review for converting the experience into knowledge."

"Under both methods, the scores of the immediate test were higher than those in experiment 1, which suggests that the participants could better memorize words in this experimental environment."

"This suggested that the participants were able to memorize and retain more English language words with the proposed method than the baseline method in the freeform learning environment."

"Although the number of forgotten words decreased compared to experiment 1, some participants still forgot the spelling of the English words similar to experiment 1."

"The time length of the memorization phase of all participants are controlled at 300 s, so statistically the result could not be calculated."

4.1.9.7 Conclusion and Future Work

"We proposed a voice-enhanced emotional flashcard application for mobile phones through which a learner can perceive the meaning of English words."

"Emotional binaural voice narrations were used to enhance L2 vocabulary learning."

"Comparing the memory enhancement effects of the voice in the proposed method with a typical voice in the baseline approach, it was found that learning by the proposed voice makes it significantly easier to remember the English word and its translation."

"Works, we will employ audio content design theory and an attention induction method to reinforce memory retention."

"Expanding the participant demographics and generalizing the results to women is also important and should be addressed in future works."

"This paper suggests that emotive story-based binaural narration promotes the memory retention of English words."

4.1.10 Theoretical Trends of Research on Technology and L2 Vocabulary Learning: A Systematic Review [74]

This is a machine-generated summary of:

Yang, Xinyuan; Kuo, Li-Jen; Eslami, Zohreh R.; Moody, Stephanie M.: Theoretical trends of research on technology and L2 vocabulary learning: A systematic review [74]

Published in: Journal of Computers in Education (2021)
Link to original: https://doi.org/10.1007/s40692-021-00187-8

If you want to cite the papers, please refer to the original.
For technical reasons we could not place the page where the original quote is coming from.

Abstract-Summary "Vocabulary development is critical for second language (L2) learners in both English as a Second Language (ESL) and English as a Foreign Language (EFL) contexts."

"A large body of research has been dedicated to how computer-assisted language learning (CALL) and mobile-assisted language learning (MALL) can facilitate vocabulary knowledge in L2 learners in both EFL and ESL settings."

"Missing from the existing research is an in-depth examination of the theories underlying vocabulary learning within technological programs."

"Understanding theoretical foundations of vocabulary learning is critical for both researchers and educators who seek to improve vocabulary development in L2 learners."

"The current study aims to close these gaps by investigating research on the use of technology for L2 vocabulary learning for learners in PreK-12 between 2011 and 2020."

"These findings suggest that research on technology-mediated vocabulary learning for Prek-12 L2 learners should be conducted from more diverse and explicit theoretical perspectives."

4.1.10.1 Introduction

"Vocabulary learning has been one of the most widely-investigated areas in technology-mediated second language acquisition (SLA) research [57–59]."

"Previous research syntheses on technology-mediated L2 learning have shown that most existing empirical studies fail to be supported by a clear theoretical approach (e.g. [58; Handley, 2014; Viberg & Gronlund, 2013)."

"Theory is a fundamental component of both research design and instructional practice, more research is needed to systematically examine what theoretical frameworks support the integration of technology in L2 vocabulary learning."

"Technology-mediated vocabulary learning has substantial potential to positively impact the vocabulary development of school-aged L2 learners."

"The purpose of the present study is to provide a comprehensive review of the theoretical trends of research on technology-mediated L2 vocabulary learning for PreK-12 L2 Learners between 2011 and 2020."

4.1.10.2 Review of Literature

"They found evidence of studies rooted in a variety of theories such as constructivism, situated learning theory, seamless language learning approach, activity theory, sociocultural theory, and theories of multimedia learning (e.g. cognitive load theory, DCT, technology acceptance model)."

"These theories were the most commonly referenced among the reviewed studies. (2) multimedia design and learning approaches, such as DCT, cognitive theory of multimedia learning, cognitive load media design principles, learning memory cycle; and (3) technology-oriented approaches, such as technology acceptance model, unified theory of acceptance and use of technology."

"Learning theories and models such as Finally, in a systematic review of CALL for vocabulary instruction among young L2 learners, Handley (2014) found that DCT, spaced learning theory, sociocultural theories, and various reading theories were the most common underlying theories."

"The purpose of the present study is to systematically examine the theoretical trends in research on the use of technology in L2 vocabulary learning among PreK-12 ELLs between 2011 and 2020."

4.1.10.3 Methods

"Titles and abstracts were then screened, upon which 240 articles were removed for one or more of the following reasons: (1) they did not target vocabulary learning (87); (2) the studies did not focus on the use of technology (52); (3) the studies examined languages other than English (12); (4) the studies were not empirical, such as literature reviews, commentaries, or book reviews (67); or, (5) the studies targeted university students and/or adults."

"The remaining articles were subject to a full review and were included if: (1) L2 vocabulary development was one of the primary outcomes; (2) the study incorporated at least one type of technology to assist L2 vocabulary learning; and (3) the study focused on PreK-12 learners of English."

"The 80 included studies were coded for the following variables: vocabulary knowledge, affordances of technology, and theoretical framework of the study."

4.1.10.4 Results

"These tools also offered students the opportunity to develop their productive vocabulary knowledge through recording their own pronunciation and receiving feedback from the instructor, or through transcribing target words [60, 61]."

"The use of captions while watching videos was emphasized to facilitate the understanding of target word meaning for EFL students [He, 2019; 62]."

"Across studies, technology was used to develop receptive vocabulary knowledge through word recognition or understanding of meaning."

"Technology was also used to facilitate learners' productive knowledge by encouraging them to use the target words for authentic purposes."

4.1.10.5 Research Question 2: What Affordances Did Technology Offer in L2 Vocabulary Learning?

"More than half of the studies (53%, n = 42) focused on multimodal learning as one of the main affordances of technology."

"Many EFL studies examined collaborative learning (n = 14) and learning motivation (n = 13) because of using technology, neither of which were emphasized in ESL contexts."

"Active knowledge making and ubiquitous learning was emphasized in studies that primarily targeted the K-5 population."

"This indicates that the portability and flexibility of mobile technology facilitated active learning, making it favorable to researchers and teachers of K-5 ELLs."

4.1.10.6 Research Question 3: What Theoretical Frameworks Have Been Used by Researchers in Technology-Integrated L2 Vocabulary Learning?

"Eighteen studies explicitly cited theories based on information/cognitive processing, such as the cognitive theory of multimedia learning and cognitive load theory to guide the design of the technology-integrated vocabulary activities."

"When the reviewed studies employed sociocognitive theories, the references were mostly implicit and emphasized learner motivation, engagement, and self-regulated vocabulary learning."

"To enhance the self-regulated vocabulary learning of fourth grade EFL students, Chen and Lee [63] incorporated data visualization and color-coded warnings into their program."

"To encourage students to practice productive vocabulary, Young and Wang [61] incorporated a game-based activity in their vocabulary learning program."

"Most of the reviewed studies reported that students had positive attitudes towards language learning upon program completion, which served as a critical indicator of the technology's success (e.g. Young & Wang [61]; Nova et al. [64])."

4.1.10.7 Discussion

"The current study examined theoretical trends of technology-integrated L2 vocabulary learning for PreK-12 ELLs between 2011 and 2020."

"It is important, as indicated in the reviewed studies, that effort has been invested in developing technology that facilitates the acquisition of productive vocabulary alongside receptive vocabulary."

"The various types of technology used in the selected studies have mainly provided multimodal presentations of information, promoted collaboration and interaction among students, and enhanced language learning motivation as well as self-regulated learning."

"The prevalence of information/cognitive theories as primary supporting theories in the current review suggests that the multimodality affordance of language learning technology is perhaps the most widely known and used by researchers and teachers."

"Many of the reviewed studies also relied on sociocognitive theories, emphasizing the influence of affective factors in the language learning process, including the need for engaging multimedia programs."

4.1.10.8 Conclusion

"This study aimed to systematically review the theoretical trends in technology-integrated L2 vocabulary learning research published between 2011 and 2020 with PreK-12 L2 learners."

"The current study fills the gap by examining studies that have utilized technology for the vocabulary learning of young L2 learners."

"This review indicates that recent studies have explored the use of technology to facilitate L2 vocabulary learning from multiple perspectives."

"The current systematic review also uncovered theoretical issues in the existing research on technology-integrated vocabulary learning for young L2 learners, which point to implications for future research."

"Future research could explore the potential of technology for L2 vocabulary learning from more diverse theoretical perspectives, extending on the multimodal features that have been widely studied and applied so far."

Bibliography

1. Nation, I. S. P. (2009). New roles for FL vocabulary? In L. Wei & V. Cook (Eds.), *Contemporary applied linguistics* (Language teaching and learning) (Vol. 1, pp. 99–116). Continuum.
2. Al-Seghayer, K. (2003). Technological and pedagogical considerations for a more effective electronic glossary. *The Reading Matrix, 3*(1), 1–15. Retrieved from http://www.readingmatrix.com/articles/al-seghayer/article.pdf
3. AbuSeileek, A. F. (2011). Hypermedia annotation presentation: The effect of location and type on the EFL learners' achievement in reading comprehension and vocabulary acquisition. *Computers & Education, 57*(1), 1281–1291.
4. Poole, R. (2012). Concordance-based glosses for academic vocabulary acquisition. *CALICO Journal, 29*(4), 679–693.
5. Yeung, A. S. (1999). Cognitive load and learner expertise: Split-attention and redundancy effects in reading comprehension tasks with vocabulary definitions. *The Journal of Experimental Education, 67*(3), 197–217.

6. Başoğlu, E. B., & Akdemir, Ö. (2010). A comparison of undergraduate students' English vocabulary learning: Using mobile phones and flash cards. *The Turkish Online Journal of Educational Technology, 9*(3), 1–7.
7. Chuang, H. Y., & Ku, H. Y. (2011). The effect of computer-based multimedia instruction with Chinese character recognition. *Educational Media International, 48*, 27–41.
8. Kim, D., & Gilman, D. A. (2008). Effects of text, audio, and graphic aids in multimedia instruction for vocabulary learning. *Educational Technology and Society, 11*, 114–126.
9. Lees, D., & Mcnee, G. (2015). Effects and impressions of digital vocabulary-learning vs. paper-based vocabulary-learning: A small-scale longitudinal study. *Kwansei Gakuin University Humanities Review, 20*, 143–164.
10. Low, J. H., Hew, S. H., & Wong, C. O. (2014). Innovative pictogram Chinese characters representation. *World Academy of Science, Engineering and Technology, 8*, 604–608.
11. Mayer, R. E. (2009). *Multimedia learning* (2nd ed.). Cambridge University Press.
12. McKenna, M. C., & Robinson, R. D. (1990). Content literacy: A definition and implications. *Journal of Reading, 34*(3), 184–186.
13. Deci, E. L., & Ryan, R. M. (2000). The "what" and "why" of goal pursuits: Human needs and the self-determination of behavior. *Psychological Inquiry, 11*(4), 227–268.
14. Reeve, J., & Jang, H. (2006). What teachers say and do to support students' autonomy during a learning activity. *Journal of Educational Psychology, 98*(1), 209.
15. Ryan, R. M., & Deci, E. L. (2006). Self-regulation and the problem of human autonomy: Does psychology need choice, self-determination, and will? *Journal of Personality, 74*(6), 1557–1586.
16. Aydin, Y. Ç., Güneri, O. Y., Yildirim, F. B., & Çag, P. (2015). Predicting college student success: College engagement and perceived English language proficiency. *Çukurova University. Faculty of Education Journal, 44*(2), 229.
17. Dörnyei, Z. (2002). The motivational basis of language learning tasks. In P. Robinson (Ed.), *Individual differences in secondary language acquisition* (pp. 137–158). John Benjamin.
18. Yang, H. (2008). On teaching strategies in second language acquisition. *US-China Education Review, 5*(1), 61–67.
19. Ibanez, M. B., Serio, A. D., Villaran, D., & Kloos, C. D. (2014). Experimenting with electromagnetism using augmented reality: Impact on flow student experience and educational effectiveness. *Computers and Education, 71*, 1–13.
20. Dede, C. (2011). Emerging technologies, ubiquitous learning, and educational transformation. In *Towards ubiquitous learning* (pp. 1–8). Springer.
21. Santos, M. E. C., Chen, A., Taketomi, T., Yamamoto, G., Miyazaki, J., & Kato, H. (2014a). Augmented reality learning experiences: Survey of prototype design and evaluation. *IEEE Transactions on Learning Technologies, 7*(1), 38–56.
22. Kaufmann, H., Schmalstieg, D., & Wagner, M. (2000). Construct3D: A virtual reality application for mathematics and geometry education. *Education and Information Technologies, 5*(4), 263–276.
23. Kaufmann, H. (2002). Construct3D: An augmented reality application for mathematics and geometry education. In *Proceedings of ACM international conference on multimedia* (pp. 656–657). ACM.
24. Billinghurst, M., & Duenser, A. (2012). Augmented reality in the classroom. *Computer, 45*(7), 56–63.
25. Mayer, R. E. (2009). *Multimedia learning*. Cambridge University Press.
26. Ogata, H., Li, M., Hou, B., Uosaki, N., & El-Bishouty, M. M. (2011). SCROLL: Supporting to share and reuse ubiquitous learning log in the context of language learning. *International Journal of Learning Technology, 5*(1), 5–24.
27. Yang, F. C. (2012). Using personalized VLS on mobile English vocabulary learning. In *Proceedings of IEEE international conference on wireless, mobile and ubiquitous technology in education* (pp. 232–234).

28. Lin, C. C., & Hsiao, H. S. (2011). The effects of multimedia annotations via PDA on EFL learners' vocabulary learning. In *Proceedings of the 19th international conference on computers in education.*
29. Cuendet, S., Bonnard, Q., Do-Lenh, S., & Dillenbourg, P. (2013). Designing augmented reality for the classroom. *Computers and Education, 68*, 557–569.
30. Sumadio, D. D., & Rambli, D. R. (2010). Preliminary evaluation on user acceptance of the augmented reality use for education. In *Proceedings of international conference on computer engineering and applications*, vol. 2 (pp. 461–465).
31. Santos, M. E. C., Chen, A., Terawaki, M., Yamamoto, G., Taketomi, T., Miyazaki, J., et al. (2013). Augmented reality X-Ray interaction in K-12 education: Theory, student perception and teacher evaluation. In *Proceedings of IEEE international conference on advanced learning technologies* (pp. 141–145).
32. Santos, M. E. C., Terawaki, M., Taketomi, T., Yamamoto, G., & Kato, H. (2015b). Development of handheld augmented reality X-ray for K-12 settings. In *Smart learning environments* (pp. 199–219). Springer.
33. Ariew, R., & Ercetin, G. (2004). Exploring the potential of hypermedia annotations for second language reading. *Computer Assisted Language Learning Journal, 17*(2), 237–259.
34. Nation, I. S. P. (2009). New roles for FL vocabulary? In L. Wei & V. Cook (Eds.), *Contemporary applied linguistics* (Vol. 1, pp. 99–116). Continuum.
35. Hulstijn, J. H., Hollander, M., & Greidanus, T. (1996). Incidental vocabulary learning by advanced foreign language students: The influence of marginal glosses, dictionary use, and reoccurrence of unknown words. *Modern Language Journal, 80*, 327–339.
36. Jacobs, G. M., Dufon, P., & Fong, C. H. (1994). L1 and L2 vocabulary glosses in L2 reading passages: Their effectiveness for increasing comprehension and vocabulary knowledge. *Journal of Research in Reading, 17*(1), 19–28.
37. Lin, J.-J., & Lin, H. (2019). Mobile-assisted ESL/EFL vocabulary learning: A systematic review and meta-analysis. *Computer Assisted Language Learning, 32*(8), 878–919. https://doi.org/10.1080/09588221.2018.1541359
38. Loewen, S., Isbell, D. R., & Sporn, Z. (2020). The effectiveness of app-based language instruction for developing receptive linguistic knowledge and oral communicative ability. *Foreign Language Annals, 53*(2), 209–233. https://doi.org/10.1111/flan.12454
39. Dörnyei, Z. (2009). *The psychology of second language acquisition*. Oxford University Press.
40. Dörnyei, Z., & Ushioda, E. (2010). *Teaching and researching motivation*. Routledge.
41. Ushioda, E., & Dörnyei, Z. (2012). Motivation. In S. M. Gass & A. Mackey (Eds.), *The Routledge handbook of second language acquisition* (pp. 396–409). Routledge.
42. Wu, Q. (2015a). Designing a smartphone app to teach English (L2) vocabulary. *Computers & Education, 85*, 170–179. https://doi.org/10.1016/j.compedu.2015.02.013
43. Wu, Q. (2015b). Pulling mobile assisted language learning (MALL) into the mainstream: MALL in broad practice. *PLoS One, 10*(5), e0128762. https://doi.org/10.1371/journal.pone.0128762
44. Coxhead, A. (2019). Academic vocabulary. In S. Webb (Ed.), *The Routledge handbook of vocabulary studies* (pp. 97–110). Routledge. https://doi.org/10.4324/9780429291586-7
45. Nation, I. S. P. (2001a). *Learning vocabulary in another language*. Cambridge University Press.
46. Nation, I. S. P. (2013). *Learning vocabulary in another language* (2nd ed.). Cambridge University Press.
47. Mofareh, A. A. (2019). The use of technology in English language teaching. *Frontiers in Education Technology, 2*(3), 168–180.
48. Bytheway, J. (2015). A taxonomy of vocabulary learning strategies used in massively multiplayer online role-playing games. *CALICO Journal, 32*(3), 508–527.
49. Gu, Y., & Johnson, R. K. (1996). Vocabulary learning strategies and language learning outcomes. *Language Learning, 46*, 643–679.
50. Weblio. (2005). Online dictionary: Weblio, Inc. http://www.weblio.jp/.

51. Goo Dictionary. (1999). Online dictionary. NTT Resonant Incorporated. https://dictionary.goo.ne.jp/.
52. Jayme Adelson-Goldstein, N. S. (2015). *Oxford picture dictionary monolingual (American English) dictionary for teenage and adult students (Oxford picture dictionary)* (2nd ed.). Oxford University Press.
53. American Heritage Dictionary. (1969). Online dictionary. Houghton Mifflin. https://ahdictionary.com/
54. mikan. (2014). *English learning application*. mikan Co., Ltd. http://mikan.link/.
55. Smart Language Apps Limited. (2015). *Learn English (US) Flashcards, English learning application*. Smart Language Apps Limited. https://itunes.apple.com/us/app/learn-english-usflashcards/id970002864?mt=8.
56. Kensinger, E. A., & Corkin, S. (2003). Memory enhancement for emotional words: Are emotional words more vividly remembered than neutral words? *Memory & Cognition, 31*(8), 1169–1180. https://doi.org/10.3758/BF03195800
57. Burston, J. (2015). Twenty years of MALL project implementation: A meta-analysis of learning outcomes. *ReCALL, 27*(1), 4–20.
58. Duman, G., Orhon, G., & Gedik, N. (2015). Research trends in mobile assisted language learning from 2000 to 2012. *ReCALL, 27*(2), 197–216.
59. Taj, I. H., Sulan, N. B., Sipra, M. A., & Ahmad, W. (2016). Impact of mobile assisted language learning (MALL) on EFL: A meta-analysis. *Advances in Language and Literary Studies, 7*(2), 76–83.
60. Fehr, C. N., Davison, M. L., Graves, F. M., Sales, C. G., Seipel, B., & Sharma, S. S. (2012). The effects of individualized, online vocabulary instruction on picture vocabulary scores: An efficacy study. *Computer Assisted Language Learning, 25*(1), 82–102.
61. Young, S. S. C., & Wang, Y. H. (2014). The game embedded CALL system to facilitate English vocabulary acquisition and pronunciation. *Journal of Educational Technology & Society, 17*(3), 239–251.
62. Lwo, L., & Lin, M. C. T. (2012). The effects of captions in teenagers' multimedia L2 learning. *ReCALL, 24*(2), 188–208.
63. Chen, Z. H., & Lee, S. Y. (2018). Application-driven educational game to assist young children in learning English vocabulary. *Journal of Educational Technology & Society, 21*(1), 70–81.
64. Nova, J. C., Chavarro, C. I. O., & Zubieta, A. M. (2017). Educational videos: A didactic tool for strengthening English vocabulary through the development of affective learning in kids. *Gist: Education and Learning Research Journal*. https://doi.org/10.26817/16925777.368
65. Lee, H., & Lee, J. H. (2014). The effects of electronic glossing types on foreign language vocabulary learning: Different types of format and glossary information. *The Asia-Pacific Education Researcher*. https://doi.org/10.1007/s40299-014-0204-3
66. Li, J.-T., & Tong, F. (2018). Multimedia-assisted self-learning materials: The benefits of E-flashcards for vocabulary learning in Chinese as a foreign language. *Reading and Writing*. https://doi.org/10.1007/s11145-018-9906-x
67. Lee, E., & Harris, R. L. W. (2018). The effects of online glossary quizzes and student autonomy on domain vocabulary learning in business law. *Journal of Computing in Higher Education*. https://doi.org/10.1007/s12528-018-9183-3
68. Santos, M. E. C., Lübke, A. I. W., Taketomi, T., Yamamoto, G., Rodrigo, M. M. T., Sandor, C., & Kato, H. (2016). Augmented reality as multimedia: The case for situated vocabulary learning. *Research and Practice in Technology Enhanced Learning*. https://doi.org/10.1186/s41039-016-0028-2
69. Akbulut, Y. (2007). Effects of multimedia annotations on incidental vocabulary learning and reading comprehension of advanced learners of English as a foreign language. *Instructional Science*. https://doi.org/10.1007/s11251-007-9016-7
70. Lee, H., Lee, H., & Lee, J. H. (2015). Evaluation of electronic and paper textual glosses on second language vocabulary learning and reading comprehension. *The Asia-Pacific Education Researcher*. https://doi.org/10.1007/s40299-015-0270-1

71. Xodabande, I., Pourhassan, A., & Valizadeh, M. (2021). Self-directed learning of core vocabulary in English by EFL learners: Comparing the outcomes from paper and mobile application flashcards. *Journal of Computers in Education*. https://doi.org/10.1007/s40692-021-00197-6
72. Ng, L. L., Azizie, R. S., & Chew, S. Y. (2021). Factors influencing ESL players' use of vocabulary learning strategies in massively multiplayer online role-playing games (MMORPG). *The Asia-Pacific Education Researcher*. https://doi.org/10.1007/s40299-021-00578-6
73. Fukushima, S. (2019). EmoTan: Enhanced flashcards for second language vocabulary learning with emotional binaural narration. *Research and Practice in Technology Enhanced Learning*. https://doi.org/10.1186/s41039-019-0109-0
74. Yang, X., Kuo, L.-J., Eslami, Z. R., & Moody, S. M. (2021). Theoretical trends of research on technology and L2 vocabulary learning: A systematic review. *Journal of Computers in Education*. https://doi.org/10.1007/s40692-021-00187-8

Chapter 5
Corpus-Based Vocabulary Studies

5.1 Machine Generated Summaries

Disclaimer: The summaries in this chapter were generated from Springer Nature publications using extractive AI auto-summarization: An extraction-based summarizer aims to identify the most important sentences of a text using an algorithm and uses those original sentences to create the auto-summary (unlike generative AI). As the constituted sentences are machine selected, they may not fully reflect the body of the work, so we strongly advise that the original content is read and cited. The auto generated summaries were curated by the editor to meet Springer Nature publication standards. To cite this content, please refer to the original papers.

Machine generated keywords: corpus, list, corpus linguistic, verb, american, analysis, japanese, discourse, speech, interface, textbook, states, united, united states, bilingual.

5.1.1 Corpus-Based Vocabulary Lists for Language Learners for Nine Languages [50]

This is a machine-generated summary of:

Kilgarriff, Adam; Charalabopoulou, Frieda; Gavrilidou, Maria; Johannessen, Janne Bondi; Khalil, Saussan; Johansson Kokkinakis, Sofie; Lew, Robert; Sharoff, Serge; Vadlapudi, Ravikiran; Volodina, Elena: Corpus-based vocabulary lists for language learners for nine languages [50]
Published in: Language Resources and Evaluation (2013)
Link to original: https://doi.org/10.1007/s10579-013-9251-2
Copyright of the summarized publication:
The Author(s) 2013

M. Udaya, C. R. Reddy (eds.), *Vocabulary, Corpus and Language Teaching*,
https://doi.org/10.1007/978-3-031-45986-3_5

If you want to cite the papers, please refer to the original.

For technical reasons we could not place the page where the original quote is coming from.

Abstract-Summary "The KELLY project and its work on developing monolingual and bilingual word lists for language learning, using corpus methods, for nine languages and thirty-six language pairs."

"The focus of the paper is thus twofold, covering pedagogical and methodological aspects of the lists' construction, and linguistic aspects of the by-product of the project, the KELLY database."

5.1.1.1 Introduction

"Word lists are much-used resources in many disciplines, from language learning to psycholinguistics."

"A natural way to develop a word list is from a corpus."

"We explore a substantial effort to generate word lists for nine languages, as far as possible in a corpus-driven, principled way, but with the overriding priority of creating lists which are as useful as possible for language learners."

"The KELLY procedure for preparing the list for each language was as follows: Identify the corpus Generate a frequency list (the 'Monolingual 1' or 'M1' list) Clean up the list, and compare it with lists from other corpora and other wordlists Make adjustments to give the 'M2' list Translate each item into all the other KELLY languages (the 'Translation 1' or 'T1' list) Use the 'back translations' to identify items for addition or deletion Make further adjustments to give the final, M3 list."

"and "What word sets of three or more words (all of different languages) are there where all words are in symmetric pairs with all others?"."

5.1.1.2 Word Lists

"Systems that use word lists in areas relating to language learning include automatic rating of good corpus examples where the vocabulary is checked for being common (frequent) versus rare (infrequent) [1–3], and readability analysis where texts are analyzed for their lexical frequency profiles [4, 5]."

"In language teaching, word frequency lists are used among other things for: defining a syllabus building graded readers deciding which words are used in: learning-to-read books for children textbooks for second language (L2) learners dictionaries language tests for L2 learners Vocabulary learning is an essential part of mastering a second language (L2)."

"In terms of language pedagogy, there are two generally accepted approaches to vocabulary learning: intentional, where activities are aimed directly at learning lexical items, such as using word lists and cards; and incidental, where learning vocabulary is a by-product of activities not primarily focused on the systematic learning of words, such as reading [6]."

5.1.1.3 Preparing the KELLY Lists

"For each language, we took the 6000 most frequent lemma + word-class pairs, and this was the M1 list, as the input to the next process. (This number is lower than the target 9000 because we expected the next steps to add many more items than they deleted, as they largely did.) This step consisted of a series of procedures to 'clean up' the list, delete anomalies, correct errors (in particular word class errors) and to check against other lists for omissions."

"Various lemmatisation errors were identified, for example the entry ty, which turned out to be an incorrect formation from ties, which should have been tie Checking unexpected verb uses which are more usefully coded as adjectives, e.g. English neighbouring rather than the verb neighbour or Polish zróżnicowany ('various') which was lemmatized as the verb zróżnicować ('vary') Amalgamating variant spellings such as organise and organize, and the Greek αυγό and αβγό ('egg'), so that their frequency is not distorted by being divided Merging and splitting, as necessary, aspectual variants of verbs and reflexive verbs, often mis-lemmatised, such as Polish opłacać się ('be worthwhile') versus opłacić ('pay for') To promote consistency between language teams, a list of word types for inclusion was drawn up at the outset."

5.1.1.4 The KELLY Database

"This is a pair of words,, of two different languages A and B, such that a translates to b and b translates to a. An example of a symmetric pair is English–Swedish and Swedish–English."

"Non-sympair-source (NSS) The other case is where b is in the source list for B. An example of an NSS is Swe–Eng: publish is in the English source list but gets the Swedish translation publicera."

"Homography across word classes, where a1 in language A is translated as b in language B, which is back-translated as a2 in A, and b is based on the same lemma/root though representing different headwords, an example of such case is Swe–Eng."

"The second subgroup relates to structural differences between languages: Word-building alternatives may give rise to a number of translation variants for the same source item."

5.1.1.5 Summary and Outlook

"We have described its work on developing word lists, monolingual and bilingual, for language learning, using corpus methods, for nine languages and 72 language pairs."

"The vocabulary has been selected firstly using objective, statistical criteria, namely the monolingual frequency lists initially generated for each language; secondly, by translating all lists into all eight other languages and investigating the network of translations in all directions to identify omissions and anomalies; thirdly, using any other corpora and wordlists that were available; and fourthly, the scrutiny of linguists."

"We investigated a sample of cases where translations were not symmetrical, and found a number of recurring patterns involving differences in the corpora, list construction methods, culture, and linguistics."

"We shall be making the case for adoption of KELLY lists (or, in all likelihood, their successors) to the language-teaching institutions of several KELLY countries."

5.1.2 To Use or Not to Use the Shorter Forms: A Corpus-Based Analysis of the Apologetic Expressions "Sorry and I'm Sorry" in American Spoken English Discourse [51]

This is a machine-generated summary of:

Arizavi, Saleh; Choubsaz, Yazdan: To Use or Not to Use the Shorter Forms: A Corpus-Based Analysis of the Apologetic Expressions "Sorry and I'm sorry" in American Spoken English Discourse [51]
Published in: Corpus Pragmatics (2018)
Link to original: https://doi.org/10.1007/s41701-018-0045-z

If you want to cite the papers, please refer to the original.
For technical reasons we could not place the page where the original quote is coming from.

Abstract-Summary "This corpus-based study explores how linguistic and socio-cognitive factors designate when, why, and how speakers say sorry and I'm sorry in two corpora of American spoken English; namely, Michigan Corpus of Academic Spoken English and Corpus of Contemporary American English."

"This study tries to cast some light on the shades of differences between sorry and I'm sorry, which seem to be taken for granted by non-native speakers of English, through analyzing one academic and one non-academic corpora."

"The results of the functional analysis suggest that most instances of the word sorry were used to indicate interruption, self-repair, and expressing regret, whereas I'm sorry was chiefly exploited to express regret and apology."

5.1.2.1 Introduction

"This requirement means that, in a corpus, only those phenomena can fully be studied whose lexical form(s) and pragmatic function(s) display a straightforward one-to-one relationship."

"To the predicament of form–function incongruities, the problem of using relatively similar expressions or some expressions and their truncated forms (e.g., sorry for I'm sorry or fine for I'm fine), which are thought to be not of much value for many speakers, might bring about different reactions if the speaker makes the wrong choice."

"What makes this study worth conducting is the meticulous concentration on the word sorry and elucidating its discourse features."

"No study has been concerned with the functions, linguistic distribution, and co-textual environment of the word sorry in one single study."

"The aim of this study is to both address the linguistic and sociocognitive bearings of the co-text in the vicinity of sorry and I'm sorry."

5.1.2.2 Backgrounds

"There are a number of studies that combine both corpus and discourse analysis, such as corpus-based discourse analyses [7], recent sociolinguistic research (e.g., Holmes & Schnurr [8]), studies in critical discourse analysis [9–12] two-pronged approach (explained later in the text)."

"What follows is a review of studies on speech acts under the banner of corpus-discourse analysis."

"Another study motivated by the notion of 'face' [13], is Diani's [14] corpus analysis of COBUILD/Birmingham spoken corpus to explore the interpretation of the formulaic I don't know with a view of the effect of intonational patterns, identify its various meanings and functions, and study the collocational patterns occurring with a number of discourse markers that influence the functions of I don't know."

"To round up this section, the present study sets out to combine the findings from corpus analysis with those from discourse analysis in the light of pragmatic and sociocognitive dimensions, hoping to secure a safe haven for bridging corpus linguistics and discourse analysis."

5.1.2.3 Method

"Our data were taken from n-grams of Corpus of Contemporary American English (COCA) and the Michigan Corpus of Academic Spoken English (MICASE)."

"The n-grams were independent of the MICASE and were accessible from the online COCA, which is the largest publicly-available, genre-balanced corpus of English—containing 520 million words."

"Are the categories of the corpus based on speech events and speech acts which pave the way for further analysis in the current study."

"In a pilot study, 25% of the corpora was extracted and manually analyzed by the first author to identify the main function played by sorry and I'm sorry and reveal the co-textual features accompanying them."

"Taking up Dörnyei's call, the current study presents a quantitative/qualitative analysis of a corpus of American spoken English, exploring the differences between distribution and collocational patterning of the expressions sorry and I'm sorry."

5.1.2.4 Results and Discussion

"The frequencies and functions of these constructions are tabulated at the end of this section. (a) $\text{Sorry}_{\text{complement}}$ [that-clause] (b) $\text{Sorry}_{\text{complement}}$ [for/about prepositional phrase] (c) $\text{Sorry}_{\text{complement}}$ [to-infinitive phrase] (d) $\text{Sorry}_{\text{complement}}$ [causative adverbial clause] (e) $\text{Sorry}_{\text{complement}}$ [a clause prefaced by a contrastive conjunction like but] (f) $\text{Sorry}_{\text{complement}}$ [an inserted turn] (g) $\text{Sorry}_{\text{complement}}$ [a proper name] Were it followed by a that-clause, sorry would serve as a marker for refusal, self-repair, reporting, and compensation (see examples 24–27, respectively)."

"Apart from those functions identified in the previous analysis based on Deutschmann's [15] classifications of apology, it was found that most instances of sorry in the three aforementioned categories were used to perform an act of self-repair, interrupting others' talk, indicating a slip of the tongue, expression of regret, introduction to a reason, expressing sympathy, as well as polite redirection and strategic rejection, whereas I'm sorry was chiefly used to suggest gaining the floor and/or maintaining one's turn in the conversation, mitigating one's wrongdoing or creating a sense of intimacy, and expressing regret."

5.1.2.5 Conclusion

"This study set out to find out how corpus linguistics can contribute to functional analysis of larger stretches of discourse like speech acts."

"As typical linguistic realizations of apology speech act, sorry and I'm sorry were chosen for the purpose of the study."

"The findings enabled the authors to conclude that the level of formality induces particular functions to the target forms sorry and I'm sorry."

"We have presented arguments to demonstrate that sorry and I'm sorry realize significantly different functions, based on frequency counts, depending on the preceding and sequential environments."

"The present study does not claim to be exhaustive, not only because it does not exclude the idea that sorry and I'm sorry are also germane in other exchanges that the corpus has not highlighted, but also because it is hard to provide clear-cut distinctions between different functions."

5.1.3 A Corpus-Based Study of Phrasal Verbs with Key Meanings in TED Talks [52]

This is a machine-generated summary of:

Liou, Hsien-Chin; Tseng, Yun-Pei: A Corpus-Based Study of Phrasal Verbs with Key Meanings in TED Talks [52]
Published in: English Teaching & Learning (2021)
Link to original: https://doi.org/10.1007/s42321-021-00101-6

If you want to cite the papers, please refer to the original.
For technical reasons we could not place the page where the original quote is coming from.

Abstract-Summary "Abstract While TED talks with their video format are popular teaching materials, limited corpus studies have been conducted to provide systematic evidence on their linguistic features."

"Following Liu and Myers' approach (2020), this study characterized the most common meaning senses of 150 PVs (Garnier and Schmitt, Language Teaching Research, 19, 645–666, 2015) among 500 TED talk transcripts based on corpus analyses with their frequency information of meaning senses."

"With contrasting analyses of PV semantic information between the TED corpus and COCA sub-corpora, we found that PVs in the TED corpus are not similar to either the COCA spoken or academic writing register (contrasted in Liu and Myers)."

"A frequency-based TED PV list was compiled as a pedagogical reference to facilitate vocabulary learning via watching TED Talks."

5.1.3.1 Introduction

"While several researchers have conducted corpus investigations into TED transcripts of video talks to help students improve their English learning, very limited studies have characterized their multi-word units using corpus analysis, especially concerning their phrasal verbs (PVs)."

"Based on two sub-corpora in COCA: spoken and academic writing (about 230 million word tokens), Liu and Myers identified and contrasted their respective meaning senses of PVs in the two registers and devised the S & AW PHaVE list."

"The purpose of this study is to conduct corpus analyses and develop a specific TED PV list based on the different key meanings of PVs."

"What are the disparities between our TED PV list and the S & AW PHaVE list concerning meaning senses of PVs which commonly appeared in the spoken or academic writing register?"

5.1.3.2 Materials and Methods of the Study

"As an extension of Liu and Myers' research and their S & AW PHaVE list (2020), we aimed to provide the most common 150 PVs (the identical set in the S & AW list) in the TED corpus with their meaning senses, meaning sense percentages as well as orders, and example sentences from our 500 TED talks."

"After automatic locating possible PVs by AntConc processing, three raters were involved to verify and compare the meaning sense of each possible PV token we located in the TED corpus against those in the S & AW PHaVE list [16] or other references."

"After three raters examined all possible PVs retrieved from TED transcripts, the PV meaning sense agreement rates among the three raters were calculated by following the formula below."

"After the TED PV list was compiled, we compared our results with those in the two registers of the S & AW PHaVE list [16], which shows meaning sense orders and percentages of each PV under either the (COCA) spoken or academic writing register."

5.1.3.3 Results

"We compared and contrasted the PV sense orders and percentages of our TED corpus with their findings in the spoken and academic writing registers respectively of the S & AW PHaVE list [16], and then classified the findings into three groups (in each division: TED-COCA spoken and TED-COCA academic writing) as defined by the same grouping method used by Liu and Myers."

"We aimed to find whether the overall PV usage concerning all their meaning sense percentages and orders in our TED corpus was closer to either the COCA spoken or its academic writing register as included in the S & AW list."

"The PV list contains 148 PV types (different phrase) based on the token (number) of meaning senses and their orders in the 500 TED talks."

5.1.3.4 Discussions

"As an extension of the S & AW PHaVE list, our TED PV list yielded a slightly different top frequency-based ten PVs concerning meaning frequency and order."

"The PV meaning senses in the S & AW PHaVE list had 90.8% coverage of all meaning senses in 148 PVs as found in our TED corpus."

"To make a PV list more specific and concise for English learners (as a second or foreign language, ESL/EFL) who may desire to acquire PV knowledge via watching TED videos, we organized the meaning senses that have occurred in the 500 TED talks by frequency and provided authentic TED sentences below each PV sense type in the TED PV list."

"Like those in the S & AW PHaVE list, the order of each meaning type for all the PVs is based on their frequency (percentage); the more often one PV occurs with its sense tokens in the TED corpus, the earlier in the order of the list where this PV is arranged."

5.1.3.5 Conclusions

"Antconc, a computer program, was adopted to locate sentences in the TED Talks that contained possible PV tokens (a lexical verb plus a particle) of 150 common PVs, same as those in the S & AW PHaVE list [16]."

"A TED PV list was compiled based on the frequency and order of meaning senses of those 148 PVs to provide ESL/EFL learners an appropriate list to look up when they use TED as English-learning materials for implicit or explicit learning."

"Like the application of the S & AW PHaVE list, our frequency-based TED PV list can be consulted by ESL/EFL learners when they watch TED talks and feel unsure of the meaning of common PVs, or by teachers or curriculum designers who desire to plan priority of instructing or assessing particular PVs over the other less common ones."

5.1.4 From Corpora to Experiments: Methodological Triangulation in the Study of Word Order at the Interfaces in Adult Late Bilinguals (L2 Learners) [53]

This is a machine-generated summary of:

Mendikoetxea, Amaya; Lozano, Cristóbal: From Corpora to Experiments: Methodological Triangulation in the Study of Word Order at the Interfaces in Adult Late Bilinguals (L2 learners) [53]

Published in: Journal of Psycholinguistic Research (2018)
Link to original: https://doi.org/10.1007/s10936-018-9560-0

If you want to cite the papers, please refer to the original.
For technical reasons we could not place the page where the original quote is coming from.

Abstract-Summary “This paper shows the need to triangulate different approaches in Bilingualism and Second Language Acquisition (SLA) research to fully understand late bilinguals’ interlanguage grammars.”

“We follow a recent line in psycholinguistic approaches to Bilingualism and SLA research (Interface Hypothesis, Sorace in Linguist Approaches Biling 1(1):1–33, 17).”

“We argue that it is precisely this multi-faceted interface approach (corpus and experimental data, core syntax and the interfaces, representational and processing models) that provides a deeper understanding of (i) the factors that favour inversion in L2 acquisition in particular and (ii) interlanguage grammars in general.”

5.1.4.1 Introduction: Interfaces in Bilingualism and SLA

“While L2 learners can successfully acquire narrow syntax properties, i.e., purely syntactic properties pertaining to the computational system, the external interfaces are highly problematic, leading to optionality, variability, and fossilization, as reported in a variety of acquisitional contexts for both child and adult bilinguals and learners with different L1-L2 combinations ([17–19] for overviews).”

“Convergence at the theoretical level can also be found in the attention given to conditions imposed on the language faculty by external interfaces, called third-factor principles in language design (which interact with the other two factors: genetic endowment and experience) within what is known as the biolinguistic approach (see Chomsky [20]).”

“The recent emphasis on the role of linguistic interfaces both in theoretical linguistics and bilingualism/SLA points towards some degrees of conceptual convergence amongst different cognitively-oriented models.”

5.1.4.2 Gathering Data for SLA Purposes

“As Myles [21: 374] states “the language produced by learners, whether spontaneously or through various elicitation procedures, remains a central source of evidence for these mental processes, and the success of SLA research therefore relies on having access to good quality data”.”

"Findings in SLA research are thus highly dependent on data collection methods."

"Relatively little use has been made of these corpora in SLA research ([21–24] for discussions)."

"SLA researchers have rightly complained that LCR is not always fully informed by SLA research [21, 23] and that large learner corpora have not been used in mainstream formal approaches to SLA [25]."

"Corpora are an invaluable tool for SLA research and researchers have recently argued for the triangulation of corpus and experimental data (e.g., Lozano and Mendikoetxea [26]; Callies [27]; Gilquin and Gries [28]; Meunier and Littre [29])."

5.1.4.3 Combining Corpus and Experimental Data in L2: S–V/ V–S Order

"The corpus data showed that learners produced XP-V–S order with unaccusatives only, in accordance to the UH experimental results, but, crucially, as we will see in the following section "The Corpus Study", the corpus data revealed previously unnoticed phenomena, namely that (i) unaccusativity is a necessary but not a sufficient condition for V–S order: S must be focus and heavy [30, 31] and that (ii) a full account of V–S structures must necessarily consider the preverbal field (XP)."

"While our initial motivation for the corpus study [31] was to test the UH in L2 grammars as manifested in previous studies and illustrated in (1), our hypotheses were not restricted to the study of the V at the lexicon-syntax interface, but focused on S at the syntax-discourse and syntax-phonology interface to fully understand the role of the interfaces in the production of Ss in postverbal ((XP-)V–S) position vs. preverbal position (S–V) in L1 Spanish–L2 English."

5.1.4.4 Discussion

"It could be argued that overproduction of it in the corpus, in contexts where we find there in native English, may be due to the high frequency of it in the input because it corresponds to different types of S: referential pronoun, expletive in weather verbs/passives/raising constructions, and anticipatory expletive in extraposed clausal Ss."

"If production of Ø with unaccusatives were an L1 transfer phenomenon, then (i) unaccusative Ø rates would be expected to be the highest, but are low across all levels and also at A1 level, when learners would be expected to transfer more; (ii) Ø rates would be predicted to be the highest for unergatives too, since heavy and focused Ss in V–S constructions appear in sentence-final position in native Spanish, independently of V type (cf. "The Corpus Study"); (iii) unaccusative Ø rates would be expected to be higher than it rates, since only the former is allowed in Spanish, but learners treat both Ø and it similarly across levels."

5.1.4.5 Conclusion

"We have shown that Bilingualism, and particularly, SLA research and LCR can benefit from two areas of convergence: (i) the triangulation of corpus and experimental data to study the same linguistic phenomenon (S–V/V–S order in L1 Spanish–L2 English); (ii) the study of how the syntactic module interfaces with other cognitive modules internal to the language faculty (lexicon-syntax interface) and external to it (syntax-discourse and syntax-phonology interfaces)."

"Though this issue has not been developed here, we pointed out in section "Introduction: Interfaces in Bilingualism and SLA" that, on the basis of third-factor principles (e.g. principles involved in language processing), convergence between two cognitive theoretical approaches (representational/generative vs. usage-based/ functional) is crucial to better understand interlanguage grammars."

"While our corpus data indicate that speakers of L1 Spanish–L2 English produce XP-V–S structures under the same interface conditions as native English speakers, future research needs to determine more precisely the ultimate cause for the difficulties encountered by learners in the syntactic encoding of XP."

5.1.5 A Corpus-Based Study of Modal Verbs in the Uniform Commercial Code of the USA [54]

This is a machine-generated summary of:

Wu, Xinyu; Li, Jian: A Corpus-Based Study of Modal Verbs in the Uniform Commercial Code of the USA [54]

Published in: International Journal for the Semiotics of Law – Revue internationale de Sémiotique juridique (2019)

Link to original: https://doi.org/10.1007/s11196-019-09620-9

If you want to cite the papers, please refer to the original.

For technical reasons we could not place the page where the original quote is coming from.

Abstract-Summary "The study specifically studies the features of modal verbs in the UCC through the comparison with the United States Code (hereinafter referred to as the USC) and Frown."

"The results show that there are significant differences between the three sets of corpora and the three main features of modal verbs in the UCC are: the high frequency use of may, the relatively lower frequency use of legal modal verb shall, and the much higher frequency of must and may not."

"With both the quantitative and qualitative analysis combining the examples, the study hopes to shed light on the related legal translation and further enhance the understanding of the modal verbs in the UCC as well as legal discourse in a more general context."

5.1.5.1 Introduction

"In the deeper economic reform, the legal language and spirit of the Uniform Commercial Code (hereinafter referred to as the UCC) of the USA is also worth learning from and it will be significant for further developing the most suitable economic regulating system for the socialism with Chinese characteristics."

"The UCC is a model code, it is enacted integrally or partially within 50 states with the goal of harmonizing the law of sales and commercial transactions across the states."

"As an important law in commercial domain in the USA, the UCC basically eliminates the barriers caused by different states' regulations on interstate transaction and greatly promotes the development of American industry and commerce."

"Many writers and editors have devoted continuous effort to revise and exhibit the UCC to the different audience in the USA, which illustrates the importance of this Code."

5.1.5.2 Modality

"As for deontic modality in Chinese legislation, scholars tended to compare the Chinese characters "ying(gai)", "(bi)xu", "ke(yi)" in legal documents to modal verbs like shall and may [32–35]."

"Cao [32] studied Chinese equivalence of modal verbs shall, may and their negation form may not or shall not in legal Chinese as a way to perform obligations, permissions, and prohibitions under the illocutionary acts theory to compare the pragmatic differences of the Chinese legal language used in Chinese mainland and Chinese Taiwan's the statutory laws."

"In Chinese legal documents, modal verbs shall and may have the highest frequency [36]."

"Further respective comparison of the modal verbs' positive and negative forms has been done by using China and Hong Kong's laws and regulations parallel corpus [37], which indicated that shall and may not were overused and misused in Chinese legal register."

5.1.5.3 Method

"This study employed quantitative and qualitative approaches to analyze the modal verbs in the Uniform Commercial Code of the USA."

"The study first chose and built up the corpora separately and carefully: Uniform Commercial Code of the USA, the other English legal documents chosen from the United States Code, and the common English language corpus Frown."

"Based on reorganization of different corpora's frequency of modal verbs, a further comparison was made between the legislations and Frown as well as between the UCC and the USC."

"The main features of the usages of the modal verbs of the Uniform Commercial Code of the USA were analyzed."

5.1.5.4 Results

"The differences between the modal verbs in three corpora will be analyzed from two levels, between the legal documents and the Frown as well as between the UCC and the USC."

"Comparing the modal verbs in legal documents, the UCC and the USC with Frown which including daily expressions, it can be noticed that can, could, might, should, need all are used more frequently in daily expression than in legal documents."

"The UCC has the highest low modal value at 59% for the high-frequently used modal verb may, even higher than the daily expression in Frown, which may indicate a more free and open context."

5.1.5.5 Discussion

"When discussing the usage features of modal verbs in the UCC, the regions and fields of legislation, the background of social relations and development must be considered."

"Since modal verb shall indicates an order, command, obligations rather than rights [33, 35, 38] and the commercial law focuses more on the rights of the common merchants and consumers, modal verb may is more suitable for illustrating the permission of a business act."

"Within the discourse domain of the UCC, besides the jurisprudential pursue of the major legal realists participated in the drafting of the UCC, the seemingly contradictory usages of different modal verbs also can be seen as a struggle and a strike for the balance between vagueness and clarity in law As Bellis [39]'s research which testified the perfect clarity in legal writing to be illusory, he concluded that we could only achieve the relative clarity by sufficient contexts under the directive thoughts of Plato, Isadore, Descartes, Locke."

5.1.5.6 Conclusion

"Since the studies on legal document are booming and legal language has its own typical features, the present study of modal verbs in the UCC, which provides an important analysis of the specific use of the modal verbs in the English commerce law in the US from sociosemiotic perspective, will undoubtedly contribute to the further understanding of modality within the legal contexts."

"The three main features of the modal verbs usages of the UCC are found: the high frequency use of may, the relatively lower frequency use of legal modal verb shall, and the much higher frequency of must and may not."

"The usages of modal verbs in the UCC may also provide a legal text as a dynamic balance between the social reality and law to explore the relative obscurity and clarity in legal language."

"The present study provides sociosemiotic interpretation of modal verbs within the context the UCC particularly."

5.1.6 Sentiment Analysis of Japanese Text and Vocabulary Learning Based on Natural Language Processing and SVM [55]

This is a machine-generated summary of:

Song, Gang: Sentiment analysis of Japanese text and vocabulary learning based on natural language processing and SVM [55]
Published in: Journal of Ambient Intelligence and Humanized Computing (2021)
Link to original: https://doi.org/10.1007/s12652-021-03040-z

If you want to cite the papers, please refer to the original.
For technical reasons we could not place the page where the original quote is coming from.

Abstract-Summary "In order to improve the effect of text sentiment classification, this study combines intelligent machine algorithms to study Japanese text sentiment classification, which provides a theoretical reference for subsequent natural language research."

"This study combines the TF-IDF algorithm with SVM to construct a Japanese text sentiment classification model and proposes a chi-square statistic that combines word frequency factor, inter-class concentration coefficient, and correction coefficient."

"Through various comparative analysis, it shows that the research model has good comprehensive performance, meets the needs of sentiment classification system, and can provide theoretical reference for related research."

5.1.6.1 Introduction

"We can extract distinguishing feature words to form feature vectors to distinguish texts with different contents."

"Before classifying Japanese text, we first need to perform word segmenting."

"It is particularly critical to find effective feature dimensionality reduction methods to further improve the accuracy and efficiency of text classification."

"In text classification, the method we generally use is to construct an evaluation function to score each feature item in the original feature space, and then arrange the scores of all feature items in ascending order to select a predetermined number of best features or set a threshold to retain those features with scores above the threshold."

"The appearance of new words reduces the accuracy of text classification, so combining new words to study text classification has practical significance [40]."

5.1.6.2 Related Work

"This is the first time sentiment has been introduced in the field of information science research."

"Sentiment computing has become a hot research field at home and abroad, mainly including sentiment feature analysis, sentiment recognition and sentiment simulation."

"The research first obtained various behavior and physiological characteristic signals caused by human emotions through various sensors, and then established an "emotional model" of the relationship between different emotions and related feature information."

"At home, the country lists "theoretical research on emotional computing in a harmonious human–machine environment" as a key project of the National Natural Science Foundation of China."

"The decision layer fusion uses different types of sensors to observe and acquire various data for the same target, and it completes the basic processing of the target information locally through each sensor."

5.1.6.3 Feature Selection Method

"It is often used in large-scale corpora, and it can remove low-frequency words that are irrelevant to categories and improve the efficiency of feature selection and the accuracy of classification."

"When the feature word has nothing to do with the category, the value of MI is 0."

"The information gain value of a feature word is used to measure the difference between the information entropy of the feature item before and after the feature word appears."

"When the feature word does not appear, its contribution to the text is less than its interference."

"When the distribution of classes and feature items is uneven, the information gain will tend to select feature words that do not appear frequently, which will result in poor classification effects."

"The greater the influence of feature items on the distribution of text categories, the greater the expected cross-entropy value [41]."

5.1.6.4 Chi-Square Statistical Algorithm

"The chi-square values of all feature words are calculated, sorted from largest to smallest, and then a certain number of words are selected as feature items."

"The disadvantage of chi-square statistics is that when there are 100 texts in a type, if the feature word appears only once in each article in this type of text set and another feature word appears 10 times in 99 articles in this type, the score calculated by the chi-square formula for the latter feature word is less than the former."

"Because the calculation formula of chi-square statistics is based on the number of texts whose feature items appear in the category, the former will be preferentially selected when sorting features, which is why low-frequency words are ignored in chi-square statistics."

"The feature word may also be selected as a feature item, and this feature word will only appear in other categories and hardly appear in its own category."

5.1.6.5 Improvement of Chi-Square Statistics

"In order to solve the problems of chi-square statistics on low-frequency word defects, uneven distribution of classes, poor classification, negative correlation between feature items and categories."

"The idea of the inter-class concentration coefficient means that the number of texts A appearing in this feature item is mostly concentrated in this category."

"When the feature item concentration degree and dispersion degree increase, the greater the correlation between the feature item and the category, the greater the number B of texts in the concentration degree."

"It can be seen that the distinguishing ability between the feature item and the category increases with the increase of A, and decreases with the increase of the number of texts B and C. The following formula is obtained by comprehensively considering A, B, and C through the correction coefficient."

"The improved method can select feature words with high frequency of feature words appearing in the text, good dispersion degree within the class, and concentrated distribution in a certain class as feature items."

5.1.6.6 TFIDF Method Combining in-Class Information Entropy

"The information distribution entropy of the feature items between categories is: When the feature item is evenly distributed within the class, the value of the information entropy among the classes reaches the maximum, and its formula is: When the feature items are more evenly distributed in each category text, the distribution of feature items between categories is inversely proportional to the contribution of feature items to the classification."

"Combining the information distribution entropy parameters within and between classes can accurately reflect the distribution of texts in inter-class and intra-class."

"The concept of entropy is introduced to characterize the distribution of feature items in intra-class."

5.1.6.7 Model Construction and Performance Analysis

"This study compares the performance of TF-IDF with BPNN model and CNN model."

"Analysis, it can be seen that the models proposed in this study have higher scores, all exceeding 95 points, which is much higher than the BPNN model and CNN model."

"In order to further verify the performance of the model, the accuracy of the Japanese text sentiment analysis is verified on the model."

"This shows that the model proposed in this study has a high recognition accuracy and can meet the performance requirements of the system."

5.1.6.8 Conclusion

"The traditional text sentiment classification mainly relies on some domain experts to classify text sentiment according to their knowledge, which is time-consuming and laborious."

"The vast majority of text sentiment classification methods use machine learning methods."

"This study combines the TF-IDF algorithm with SVM to construct a Japanese text sentiment classification model and proposes a chi-square statistic that combines word frequency factor, inter-class concentration coefficient, and correction co-efficient."

"Through various comparative analysis, it shows that the research model has good comprehensive performance, meets the needs of sentiment classification system, and can provide theoretical reference for related research."

5.1.7 Gender Construction in the Indonesian Government-Distributed English Textbook: Combining Critical Discourse Analysis and Corpus Linguistics [56]

This is a machine-generated summary of:

Suwarno, None; Triyono, Sulis; Ashadi, None; Sahayu, Wening: Gender Construction in the Indonesian Government-Distributed English Textbook: Combining Critical Discourse Analysis and Corpus Linguistics [56]
Published in: Sexuality & Culture (2021)
Link to original: https://doi.org/10.1007/s12119-021-09870-5

If you want to cite the papers, please refer to the original.
For technical reasons we could not place the page where the original quote is coming from.

Abstract-Summary "Many studies on gender in English language textbooks have been much reported under the umbrella of critical discourse studies."

"In response to this gap, the present discourse study adopted corpus linguistics and critical micro-semiotic analysis to investigate the representation of gender in the English as a foreign language (EFL) textbook used in Indonesian junior high schools [9]."

"Based on the corpus linguistic analysis, findings showed that the textbook writers constructed gender fairness by including gender-neutral vocabularies in both verbal and visual texts in order to avoid gender-marked words."

"The practical implication of the present study is that English teachers and language textbook designers should be fully aware of the interplay between language and gender issues to minimise gender misconceptions when writing language textbooks."

5.1.7.1 Introduction

"Adopting a corpus linguistic study, Lee [42] reported the representation of gender in written texts of four EFL textbooks series geared for Japanese high school students published in 2011."

"Another Indonesian discourse study [42] explored the portrayal of women in gendered visual and textual discourses in EFL textbooks taught to senior high schools students (Grades 10–12)."

"A recent critical discourse study of gender in English textbooks for junior high schools in Indonesia (Grades 7 and 8) was undertaken to investigate the female representation [42]."

"The present study addresses the following specific research questions: (1) What is the proportion of males and females both textually and visually represented in the selected textbook? (2) Are there gender equality constructions in verbal and visual texts of the selected textbook? (3) Are there gender stereotypes depicted through textual and visual illustrations in the textbook examined?"

5.1.7.2 The Study

"The present study aims to elucidate how gendered discourses of written texts and visual illustrations were constructed in an EFL textbook currently taught to the Indonesian junior high school students."

"This allows for a more comprehensive analysis of gendered discourses in the textbook examined in terms of both lexical and visual choices."

"Drawing on an open corpus search software tool, AntConc [43] was employed to undertake computational analysis of gendered lexes presented in the selected textbook."

"Critical micro-semiotic analysis was used to examine verbal and pictorial texts containing a myriad values, including gender stereotyping or mainstreaming [44]."

"We also adopted van Leeuwen's [42] theory regarding the aspects of social practices to identify and analyse the gendered discourses in verbal and visual illustrations."

"Discursive analysis was undertaken to examine the portrayal of gender multimodally presented in the selected textbook."

5.1.7.3 Findings and Discussion

"The analyses began by calculating male and female vocabularies in terms of gendered characters and pronouns."

"Further, grounded in Law and Chan [42], the proportion of female and male characters in visual images was categorised into five types: male-monopolised (portrayed with men only), female-monopolised (portrayed with women only), male-dominated (depicted more men), female-dominated (depicted more women), and gender-shared (men and women are equally represented)."

"It might be intended to avoid a gender-marked word by replacing the proper names of male and female who play the role of students."

"The present empirical evidence demonstrates a traditional stereotype that domestic chores as social practices are considered to feminine work as well as echoes earlier gender-based discourse studies [42, 45]."

"The empirical evidence indicates that the textbook authors constructed gender stereotypes in terms of sports and reading."

5.1.7.4 Conclusion

"Regarding the frequency of gendered textual and visual discourses and the best words choice in order to achieve gender fairness, the findings show that the authors are fully aware of minimising gender inequality."

"The selected textbook contains visual artifacts that show gender equity pertinent to the number of male and female characters that appear together in a picture."

"Regarding, the frequency of gendered words occurrences, though the degree of female domination appeared in the textbook, the overall ratio was relatively balanced."

"Further, it is expected that the present findings could provide curriculum designers, textbook authors, and English teachers with a better understanding of the interplay between language and gender in order to minimise gender misconceptions."

"We suggest that any language textbooks should promote gender fairness."

5.1.8 Suggestions for Vocabulary Focused Reading Lessons for Mainstream Classrooms Addressing Both L1 and L2 Learners [57]

This is a machine-generated summary of:

Seifert, Susanne; Kulmhofer, Andrea; Paleczek, Lisa; Schwab, Susanne; Gasteiger-Klicpera, Barbara: Suggestions for Vocabulary Focused Reading Lessons for Mainstream Classrooms Addressing Both L1 and L2 Learners [57]

Published in: Early Childhood Education Journal (2016)
Link to original: https://doi.org/10.1007/s10643-015-0762-x

If you want to cite the papers, please refer to the original.

For technical reasons we could not place the page where the original quote is coming from.

Abstract-Summary "The increasing number of second language learners in classrooms all around the world has required teachers to adapt their teaching methods and materials to the various learners' needs."

"Language learners in particular need specific learning strategies, which not only aim at helping them understand the linguistic structure of the language of instruction, but also enable them to remember and comprehend the many different words in this "foreign" language."

"For second language learners, developing reading skills and improving language abilities need to go hand in hand independent of the language."

"This article presents suggestions for reading lessons emphasizing vocabulary for both first and second language learners of various linguistic backgrounds."

5.1.8.1 Introduction

"Vocabulary knowledge has a greater impact on the reading development of L2 learners than on readers who acquire reading competencies in their L1 [46]."

"Nation [47] sees insufficient vocabulary knowledge as one of the major barriers to reading acquisition for L2 learners."

"Reading teachers can support L2 learners in their process of learning to read through vocabulary building."

"Vocabulary building represents one of the main pillars reading lessons should be based on—not only for L2 learners, but also for L1 children, particularly when they come from families of low socioeconomic backgrounds [48, 49]."

"This article provides suggestions for vocabulary focused reading lessons appropriate for classrooms with L1 and L2 learners independent of the language of instruction."

"Twelve classrooms with a comparable amount of L2 learners receiving traditional reading instruction served as a control group."

5.1.8.2 Organizing Vocabulary Building Around Topics

"During the process, the teacher needs to pay attention whether all the vocabulary words chosen for the topic have been mentioned by the students."

"If not all the vocabulary words were mentioned by the students, the teacher can then introduce them by describing what they mean and by highlighting the corresponding scene in the topic picture."

"Such programs and applications can be quite helpful for vocabulary learning as they allow the students to enter the relevant vocabulary words and practice them in various contexts not only in school, but also at home."

"Clues for the missing vocabulary words must be found in the original version of the text the student read."

"The student needs to think about the vocabulary words, needs to re-read if unsure which word is missing and at the same time write the word."

"For some L2 learners, the texts might contain more difficult words than can be covered by the topic-related vocabulary."

5.1.8.3 Summary

"To face these challenges, teachers need tools that support them in adapting reading lessons to the various learners' needs."

"Integrating vocabulary building and providing rich and robust vocabulary instruction in reading classes is one essential approach to address the learning needs of both L1 and L2 learners."

"For teaching reading to L2 learners, vocabulary building is even more important because these students need to increase their L2 vocabulary to keep pace with their native speaking peers."

Bibliography

1. Kilgarriff, A., Husák, M., McAdam, K., Rundell, M., & Rychlý, P. (2008). GDEX: Automatically finding good dictionary examples in a corpus. In E. Bernal & J. DeCesaris (Eds.), *Proceedings of the XIII EURALEX international congress* (pp. 425–432). Universitat Pompeu Fabra.
2. Kosem, I., Husák, M., & McCarthy, D. (2011). GDEX for Slovene. In I. Kosem & K. Kosem (Eds.), *Proceedings of eLex 2011 on electronic lexicography in the 21st century: New applications for new users, Bled, 10–12 November 2011* (pp. 151–159). Trojina, Institute for Applied Slovene Studies.
3. Borin, L., Forsberg, M., Friberg Heppin, K., Johansson, R., & Kjellandsson, A. (2012). Search result diversification methods to assist lexicographers. In *Proceedings of the 6th linguistic annotation workshop.*
4. Heimann Mühlenbock, K. (2012). *I see what you mean—Assessing readability for specific target groups* (PhD thesis). Department of Swedish, University of Gothenburg.
5. Volodina, E. (2010). *Corpora in language classroom: Reusing Stockholm Umeå corpus in a vocabulary exercise generator*. LAP Lambert Academic Publishing.
6. Nation, I. S. P. (2001). *Learning vocabulary in another language*. Cambridge University Press.
7. Baker, P. (2006). *Using corpora in discourse analysis*. Continuum.
8. Holmes, J., & Schnurr, S. (2005). Politeness, humor and gender in the workplace: Negotiating norms and identifying contestation. *Journal of Politeness Research: Language, Behaviour, Culture, 1*(1), 121–149.
9. Fairclough, N. (2000). *New labor, new language?* Routledge.
10. Barker, C., & Galasińksi, D. (2001). *Cultural studies and discourse analysis: A dialogue on language and identity*. Sage.
11. Mautner, G. (2008). Analyzing newspapers, magazines and other print media. In R. Wodak & M. Krzyżanowski (Eds.), *Qualitative discourse analysis for the social sciences* (pp. 30–53). Palgrave Macmillan.
12. Matthiessen, C. M. (2006). Frequency profiles of some basic grammatical systems: An interim report. In S. Hunston & G. Thompson (Eds.), *System and corpus: Exploring connections* (pp. 103–142). Equinox.
13. Goffman, E. (1967). *Interaction ritual: Essays in face-to-face behavior*. Doubleday & Company Inc.
14. Diani, G. (2004). The discourse functions of I don't know in English conversation. In K. Ajmir & A. Stenström (Eds.), *Discourse patterns in spoken and written corpora* (pp. 157–173). John Benjamins.
15. Deutschmann, M. (2003). *Apologizing in British English*. Umea University.

16. Liu, D., & Myers, D. (2020). The most-common phrasal verbs with their key meanings for spoken and academic written English: A corpus analysis. *Language Teaching Research, 24*(3), 403–424.
17. Sorace, A. (2011). Pinning down the concept of "interface" in bilingualism. *Linguistic Approaches to Bilingualism, 1*(1), 1–33.
18. White, L. (2009). Grammatical theory: Interfaces and L2 knowledge. In W. C. Ritchie & T. K. Bhatia (Eds.), *The new handbook of second language acquisition* (pp. 49–68). Bingley.
19. White, L. (2011). Second language acquisition at the interfaces. *Lingua, 121*(4), 577–590.
20. Chomsky, N. (2005). Three factors in language design. *Linguistic Inquiry, 36*(1), 1–22.
21. Myles, F. (2005). Interlanguage corpora and second language acquisition research. *Second Language Research, 21*(4), 373–391.
22. Myles, F. (2007). Using electronic corpora in SLA research. In D. Ayoun (Ed.), *Handbook of French applied linguistics* (pp. 377–400). John Benjamins.
23. Myles, F. (2015). Second language acquisition theory and learner corpus research. In S. Granger, G. Gilquin, & F. Meunier (Eds.), *The Cambridge handbook of learner corpus research* (pp. 309–332). Cambridge University Press.
24. Rutherford, W., & Thomas, M. (2001). The child language data exchange system in research on second language acquisition. *Second Language Research, 17*(2), 195–212.
25. Lozano, C., & Mendikoetxea, A. (2013b). Learner corpora and second language acquisition: The design and collection of CEDEL2. In A. Díaz-Negrillo, N. Ballier, & P. Thompson (Eds.), *Automatic treatment and analysis of learner corpus data* (pp. 65–100).
26. Lozano, C., & Mendikoetxea, A. (2013a). Corpus and experimental data: Subjects in second language research. In S. Granger, G. Gilquin, & F. Meunier (Eds.), *Twenty years of learner corpus research: Looking back, moving ahead*. Presses Universitaires de Louvain.
27. Callies, M. (2009). *Information highlighting in advanced learner English: The syntax-pragmatics interface in second language acquisition*. John Benjamins.
28. Gilquin, G., & Gries, S. T. (2009). Corpora and experimental methods: A state-of-the-art review. *Corpus Linguistics and Linguistic Theory, 5*(1), 1–26.
29. Meunier, F., & Littre, D. (2013). Tracking learners' progress: Adopting a dual "corpus cum experimental data" approach. *The Modern Language Journal, 97*(S1), 61–76.
30. Lozano, C., & Mendikoetxea, A. (2008). Postverbal subjects at the interfaces in Spanish and Italian learners of L2 English: A corpus analysis. In G. Gilquin, S. Papp, & M. B. Díez-Bedmar (Eds.), *Linking up contrastive and learner corpus research* (pp. 85–125). Rodopi.
31. Lozano, C., & Mendikoetxea, A. (2010). Interface conditions on postverbal subjects: A corpus study of L2 English. *Bilingualism: Language and Cognition, 13*(4), 475–497.
32. Cao, D. (2009). Illocutionary acts of Chinese legislative language. *Journal of Pragmatics, 41*, 1329–1340.
33. Cheng, L., & Sin, K. K. (2011). A sociosemiotic interpretation of linguistic modality in legal settings. *Semiotica, 185*(1/4), 123–146.
34. Li, J., Cheng, L., & Cheng, W. (2016). Deontic meaning making in legislative discourse. *Semiotica, 209*, 323–340.
35. Li, K. X. (2007). The function and translation of the central modal verbs in English legal texts. *Chinese Translators Journal, 6*, 54–60.
36. Yang, X. Z. (2006). English modality and text types. *Foreign Languages and Their Teaching, 1*, 1–4.
37. Wang, Z. Y. (2013). A comparative study of modal verbs shall and may's translation in legal texts. *Shanghai Journal of Translators, 4*, 52–57.
38. Cheng, W., & Cheng, L. (2014). Epistemic modality in court judgments: A corpus-driven comparison of civil cases in Hong Kong and Scotland. *English for Specific Purposes, 33*, 15–26.
39. Bellis, D. (2016). The illusion of clarity: A critique of 'pure' clarity using examples drawn from judicial interpretations of the constitution of the United States. In A. Wagner & C. F. Sophie (Eds.), *Obscurity and clarity in the law: Prospects and challenges* (pp. 197–219). Routledge.
40. Goode, B. (2002). Voice over internet protocol (VoIP). In *Proceedings of IEEE* (pp. 1495–1517).

41. Wang, Y., Xie, Z., Xu, K., Dou, Y., & Lei, Y. (2016). An efficient and effective convolutional auto-encoder extreme learning machine network for 3D feature learning. *Neurocomputing, 174*, 988–998.
42. Eagly, A. H., Nater, C., Miller, D. I., Kaufmann, M., & Sczesny, S. (2020). Gender stereotypes have changed: A cross-temporal meta-analysis of US public opinion polls from 1946 to 2018. *American Psychologist, 75*(3), 301–351. https://doi.org/10.1037/amp0000494
43. Anthony, L. (2020). AntConc (Version 3.5.9) [Computer Software]. Tokyo: Waseda University. Retrieved from https://www.laurenceanthony.net/software
44. Mengistie, S. M., & Worku, M. Y. (2021). Gender representation in educational materials: A focus on Ethiopian English textbooks. In W. L. Filho, A. M. Azul, L. Brandli, A. L. Salvia, & T. Wall (Eds.), *Gender equality, encyclopedia of the UN sustainable development goals* (pp. 599–611). Springer.
45. Barton, A., & Sakwa, L. N. (2012). The representation of gender in English textbooks in Uganda. *Pedagogy, Culture & Society, 20*(2), 173–190. https://doi.org/10.1080/02188791.2014.924388
46. Verhoeven, L. (2000). Components in early second language reading and spelling. *Scientific Studies of Reading, 4*(4), 313–330.
47. Nation, I. S. P. (1995/1996). Best practice in vocabulary teaching and learning. *EA Journal, 3*(2), 7–15.
48. Rupley, W. H., Logan, J. W., & Nichols, W. D. (1998/1999). Vocabulary instruction in a balanced reading program. *The Reading Teacher, 52*(4), 336–346.
49. Cassidy, J., & Cassidy, D. (2005/2006). What's hot, what's not for 2006. *Reading Today, 23*(1), 8–9.
50. Kilgarriff, A., Charalabopoulou, F., Gavrilidou, M., Johannessen, J. B., Khalil, S., Johansson Kokkinakis, S., et al. (2013). Elena corpus-based vocabulary lists for language learners for nine languages. *Language Resources and Evaluation, 48*, 121–163. https://doi.org/10.1007/s10579-013-9251-2
51. Arizavi, S., & Choubsaz, Y. (2018). To use or not to use the shorter forms: A corpus-based analysis of the apologetic expressions "sorry and I'm sorry" in American spoken English discourse. *Corpus Pragmatics, 3*, 21–47. https://doi.org/10.1007/s41701-018-0045-z
52. Liou, H.-C. (2021). Tseng, Yun-Pei a corpus-based study of phrasal verbs with key meanings in TED talks. *English Teaching & Learning, 46*, 395–415. https://doi.org/10.1007/s42321-021-00101-6
53. Mendikoetxea, A., & Lozano, C. (2018). From corpora to experiments: Methodological triangulation in the study of word order at the interfaces in adult late bilinguals (L2 learners). *Journal of Psycholinguistic Research, 47*, 871–898. https://doi.org/10.1007/s10936-018-9560-0
54. Wu, X., & Li, J. (2019). A corpus-based study of modal verbs in the uniform commercial code of the USA. *International Journal for the Semiotics of Law, 32*, 463–483. https://doi.org/10.1007/s11196-019-09620-9
55. Song, G. (2021). Sentiment analysis of Japanese text and vocabulary learning based on natural language processing and SVM. *Journal of Ambient Intelligence and Humanized Computing*. https://doi.org/10.1007/s12652-021-03040-z
56. Suwarno, N., Triyono, S., Ashadi, N., & Sahayu, W. (2021). Gender construction in the Indonesian government-distributed English textbook: Combining critical discourse analysis and corpus linguistics. *Sexuality & Culture, 25*, 2158–2175. https://doi.org/10.1007/s12119-021-09870-5
57. Seifert, S., Kulmhofer, A., Paleczek, L., Schwab, S., & Gasteiger-Klicpera, B. (2016). Suggestions for vocabulary focused reading lessons for mainstream classrooms addressing both L1 and L2 learners. *Early Childhood Education Journal, 45*, 333–345. https://doi.org/10.1007/s10643-015-0762-x

Chapter 6
Conclusion

Vocabulary learning has long been considered as one of the essential components for developing language learning, Many strategies are integrated to enhance vocabulary acquisition. Subsequently, the current volume presents research that investigates vocabulary acquisition and the strategies employed by teachers and learners. The teaching process can be motivating and interesting with the help of ICT as it offers a helping hand in different domains of ELT. In addition, the discussions also remind current researchers that more attention and effort should be paid to ICT and CALL studies, along with Corpus.

The relationship between corpus and L2 teaching is an emerging field of applied corpus linguistics and sketches avenues for future research activities that may positively impact L2 teaching. We hope to have shown that corpus resources and methods have great potential to improve pedagogical practise and that corpora can be used in a number of ways, indirectly to inform teaching materials and reference works and directly as language learning tools and repositories for the design of data-intensive teaching activities. I have also tried to make it clear that a lot still remains to be done in research and practise before corpora will eventually arrive in the classroom. There needs to be a lot more communication between corpus researchers and practitioners so that teachers and students get the help they need in future.

M. Udaya, C. R. Reddy (eds.), *Vocabulary, Corpus and Language Teaching*,
https://doi.org/10.1007/978-3-031-45986-3_6

GPSR Compliance
The European Union's (EU) General Product Safety Regulation (GPSR) is a set of rules that requires consumer products to be safe and our obligations to ensure this.

If you have any concerns about our products, you can contact us on

ProductSafety@springernature.com

In case Publisher is established outside the EU, the EU authorized representative is:

Springer Nature Customer Service Center GmbH
Europaplatz 3
69115 Heidelberg, Germany

www.ingramcontent.com/pod-product-compliance
Ingram Content Group UK Ltd.
Pitfield, Milton Keynes, MK11 3LW, UK
UKHW020821290926
15470UKWH00003B/1298
* 9 7 8 3 0 3 1 4 5 9 8 5 6 *